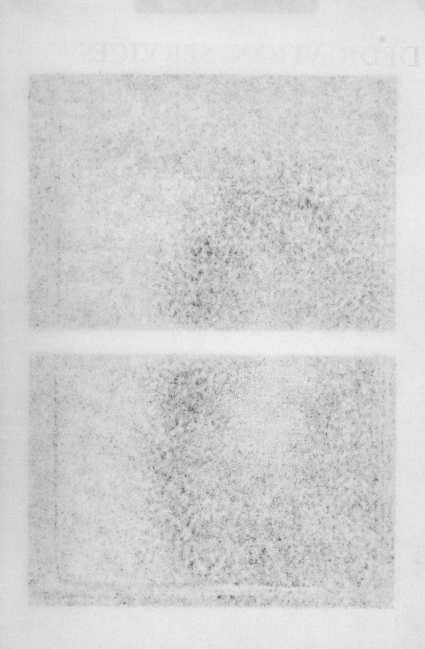

DEDICATION SERVICES

by
Samuel Ward Hutton

BAKER BOOK HOUSE
Grand Rapids, Michigan
1964

Library of Congress Catalog Card Number: 64-8349

PHOTOLITHOPRINTED BY CUSHING - MALLOY, INC.
ANN ARBOR, MICHIGAN, UNITED STATES OF AMERICA
1964

INTRODUCTION

The busy pastor has many needs for resources, but few of them can be so pressing and urgent as the need for a body of material to which he may turn for help and guidance in the many experiences of worship in which "persons, places, and things," are to be dedicated.

Samuel Ward Hutton is a master of this field as few persons in this generation have proved to be. A teacher of worship over a period of many years in Texas Christian University, Mr. Hutton has spent many hours collecting, reviewing, editing, and creating worship materials that have to do with these experiences of dedication. The fruit of these long years of intelligent and consecrated labor is presented in this volume. The book is neatly divided into three major classifications, making the material easily available. The simple, but quite accurate format by which the work is divided into dedications of "persons, places, things," is itself an index into the orderly mind of the author and editor of this work.

This book should be in every minister's library and available to the Worship Committees of the churches. I am pleased to have a part in sending this work on what must prove to be a valuable mission to the worship experience of Christian communities throughout the world.

Granville T. Walker, Minister
University Christian Church,
Fort Worth, Texas

PREFACE

It is the purpose of this book to make available in one volume materials suitable for a wide variety of dedication services. The aim is to guide, to stimulate initiative, and to provide a ready reference for those who are called upon to prepare for dedication of "persons, places, things".

There is much of the personal element, local color, appropriateness to the occasion, to be considered in relation to each dedication service whether elaborate or quite simple. Each service should be "tailor made". A "hand-me-down" is far from adequate. The service must be real, packed with worship values, free from excessive verbiage, sincere and overflowing with meaning.

Conscious that interest in the dedication idea is steadily increasing, this volume seeks to meet the growing opportunity all along the entire gamut of Christian experience by providing sample, completed programs, following an organized pattern, and to provide additional source material for high quality leadership initiative.

Outstanding institutions, special events, recognition of personal and group achievement, and significant evidences of progress need to be pointed up so that due recognition may be given and the experience shared with others. This, it seems, is good psychology, and it pays to do it right.

It is not possible to give individual credit to everyone who has in someway contributed to the contents of this volume. Where the source of certain services or portions thereof is known, due credit is given, and along with this, our sincere appreciation is hereby expressed.

The materials gathered, adapted, and used in this book have come from many individuals representing several religious communions and reveal a cross-section of the prevailing practices common to these church groups.

The compiler is under definite obligation to Miss Golda Wilhite for painstaking care in reading, correcting and copying the manuscript looking toward publication. Advice and suggestions from personal friends of long standing have added much to the enrichment of this volume.

All quotations of Scripture used are from the Revised Standard Version of the Bible. These are used by permission of the copyright owners, the National Council of the Churches of Christ in the United States and Canada. We are deeply grateful for this generous cooperation.

If, in any way, an unauthorized item appears in this volume, abject apology is offered. In our eagerness to make these materials available to Christian leadership everywhere some needed notation regarding source may have been omitted.

S. W. Hutton

TABLE OF CONTENTS

Part I

DEDICATION OF PERSONS

Dedication of Parent and Child 9

Dedication of a Child 10

Dedication of Youth 11

An Installation Service for a Youth Group 13

A Candlelight Commissioning Service 15

A Dedication Service for a Men's Group 17

A Service of Worship and Dedication of Women 18

An Installation Service for a Women's Group 20

A Church Leadership Recognition Service 21

A Service of Leadership Dedication 22

A Service of Recognition and Dedication for Church School

Leaders 23

A Leadership Dedication Ritual 24

A Charge to a Young Minister 25

A Charge to the Congregation Ordaining a Young Minister . 26

A Service of Installation and Dedication of a Minister . . 29

Installation of a Minister of Music 31

A Choir Dedication Service 33

Suggestions Pointing the Way toward Dedication of Persons . 35

Part II

DEDICATION OF PLACES

Dedication of a Church Building Site 39

A Ground Breaking Service 41

A Cornerstone Laying Service 42

Dedication of an Educational Building 44

Service for an Anniversary of the Dedication of a Church
    Building 45

Dedication of a Church Sanctuary 47

Dedication of a New Addition to a Church Plant 49

Dedication of a House of Worship 50

Dedication of a Church Camp 51

Dedication of a Business Establishment 54

Dedication of a Home 55

Service for a Mortgage Burning 57

Farewell Service for an Old Church Building 59

Part III

DEDICATION OF THINGS

Dedication of an Organ 63

Dedication of a Service 64

Dedication of the Cross 65

Dedication of a Pulpit Bible 65

Dedication of New Communion Ware 66

Dedication of American and Christian Flags 67

Dedication of a Baptistry 69

Dedication of a Piano 70

Dedication of a Hymnal 71

Dedication of Church Pews 73

Dedication of Chimes 75

Dedication of a Pulpit 76

Dedication of an Art Glass Window 78

Dedication of Church Funds 79

PART I

DEDICATION OF PERSONS

DEDICATION OF PARENT AND CHILD

"Next to individual Christian character, Christianity's greatest achievement and its most signal triumph has been in the creation of the Christian home."

— W. C. Morre

The different religious communions are giving increasing emphasis to the underlying values in the dedication of parent and child. The prevailing practice of some communions includes the rite of infant baptism within this dedication. This rite is entirely omitted in others. Sometimes the experience is designated as the blessing of little children, but a preferable designation would seem to be the dedication of parent and child. This places upon the parent a recognized responsibility for the nurture and training of his offspring.

A public service of dedication links the home with the church in sharing this joint responsibility and places the "child in the midst" in keeping with the thought, word and deed of the Master Teacher.

A beautiful, appropriate printed service for the dedication, or blessing of parent and child, may be purchased from the publisher of your choice. Then the actual copy you use in the public service may be signed by minister and parents, and kept by the parents as a record and reminder of this Christian worship experience. Usually these beautifully designed services are printed in the form of a booklet

In one church ten babies were dedicated, along with their parents, to Christ and his Church in a thrilling service at the morning hour of worship. This service was arranged and conducted by the minister. It was an adorable, inspiring sight, and emotions ran at high tide. As the choir and congregation sang two stanzas of "I Think when I Read that Sweet Story of Old," the minister stepped to the center of the chancel, and the parents with babes in arms came forward to the chancel steps.

The name of each child was called along with the name of each parent. A word of blessing was spoken in behalf of each child, and each mother was presented with a fragrant red rose. A meaningful prayer of dedication and blessing followed. In the printed order of worship for the morning the names of the babies and their parents were listed. As the choir and congregation sang the last stanza of the same hymn mentioned above the parents and their priceless treasures returned to their seats, or to the church nursery.

"Idols of the Hearth" makes a very appropriate sermon subject for the occasion. Such an experience is unforgettable. It is a worthy strategy, based on sound psychology, which pays top dividends in Christian education.

DEDICATION OF A CHILD

MINISTER: "They brought young children to Christ, that he should touch them; and his disciples rebuked those that brought them. But when Jesus saw it, he was much displeased, and said unto them, Suffer the little children to come unto me, and forbid them not; for of such is the Kingdom of God. Verily I say unto you, Whosoever shall not receive the Kingdom of God as a little child, he shall not enter therein. And he took them up in his arms, put his hands upon them, and blessed them." — Mark 10:13-16.

Dearly beloved, the divine-human task of developing a personality after the birth of a child is the most delicate and serious work to which man is called. All the sights and sounds that play upon the sensitive little body help to determine his future characteristics. The love of the home affects the child in a thousand ways for good. As the child grows he may receive the spiritual life of his parents as a rose drinks in the sunlight. The religious conversation of a mother with her child, even at a very tender age, will make for his fuller and richer growth. God will have access to your child if you will keep the doors of your own lives open to Him. If the child does not absorb the beautiful sense of God during the first critical period of the development of his personality, usually he will find the sense of God dim when he is grown up, and much more difficult to acquire.

Religion is natural to the human heart, and is, therefore, as much a part of the child's nature as are his dependence on his parents and his trust in them. It is your duty, therefore, to receive this child from God's hand and to teach *him* to know and love God, and, working in obedience to God's will to help in the unfolding of the child's spiritual life. From your example the child must learn to pray. From your example *he* must learn to read and love the Bible, and from your example *he* must learn the way of fellowship with Christ.

Above all, you are to make it your constant prayer and effort to lead the child to know and love Christ so that when *he* comes to the age of proper understanding *he* will choose of *his* own will to confess Christ as *his* Saviour, to obey Him, and to give *himself* in loyal and loving service as a member of the Church, which is the Body of Christ. Do you, Mr. and Mrs. .... promise to pray for and with this child for *his* growth in knowledge of God, and in the spiritual life?

PARENTS: We do.

MINISTER: Do you promise to train this child in body, mind, and soul for service to and fellowship with God?

PARENTS: We do.

MINISTER: Do you promise to do all you can to lead *him* at the proper age to confess *his* faith in Christ?

PARENTS: We do.

MINISTER: What is the name of this child?

PARENTS: The name of this child is ....

MINISTER: The name of this child is ....

MINISTER: Let us pray.

O Lord, gracious and merciful, grant us Thy blessing as we wait before Thee. Teach these, Thy servants, the sacredness of parenthood, and the beauty of home life. Help them to see in this Child an opportunity from Thee, and help them so to walk before Thee that these tender feet may find the path of faith, trust, justice, honour, and righteousness. Give them patience, wisdom, judgment and heavenly favour in their task. Bless this Child O Lord, with strength of body, mind, and soul; and grant that the growth of this Child may ever be toward Thee; through Jesus Christ our Lord. Amen.

MINISTER: The Lord bless thee, and keep thee;
The Lord make His face shine upon thee, and be gracious unto thee;
The Lord lift up His countenance upon thee and give thee peace;
Both now and in the life everlasting. Amen.

(Available through the Bethany Press, Box 179, Main Post Office, St. Louis, Mo.)

DEDICATION OF YOUTH

ORGAN, OR PIANO MUSIC
HYMN: "Are Ye Able, Said the Master" (all stanzas)
SCRIPTURE READING: Ecclesiastes 11:9, I Samuel 18:1-5; II Timothy 1:13-14

PRAYER HYMN: "I Would Be True" (Stanzas 1,2)
PRAYER
PRAYER HYMN: "I Would Be True" (Stanza 3)
SPECIAL MUSIC   (A youth group)
MESSAGE: "Rejoice in Thy Youth" (Minister)
HYMN: "Give of Your Best to the Master"
LITANY OF DEDICATION

Leader: To the end that every growing experience of the days of our youth may be an expression of Thy will being done on earth;

That our friends, homes, school, church, nation and world may be touched by Thy hand working in us,

People: We dedicate ourselves to the principles and ideals of Jesus Christ.

Leader: That the energy which quickens the muscles and nerves of our bodies may move to the defense of all that is good;

That the skill and toil of our hands may create new beauty and usefulness for all men;

That the capacity for new life divinely granted may ever be a sharing of Thy eternal continuation of the human race,

People: We dedicate our physical selves with their sensations of strength, weariness, pleasure and pain to Thy work and toil among our fellow men.

Leader: In the hope that our searching and study may reveal more of Thee and may present to us insights for the betterment of every nation;

With the conviction that contemplation of the past and present may guide us in making troublesome decisions in accordance with Thy will;

Desiring to exercise our reason that prejudice and ignorance may vanish;

In trust that our imaginations may form plans for self, home, and community upon Thy foundations.

People: We give Thee our mental selves with their powers of thinking, reasoning, studying, and planning.

Leader: That our sweeping emotions which carry us to love and hate alike may bring us only to love of all men;

That our binding friendships may unite young lives in a spirit of sharing;

That we may aspire to the high goals of life;

That our hearts may be filled with compassion for the oppressed of the world, moving our hands to acts of service,

People: We dedicate our emotional selves with their compassion and anger, distress and happiness to Thine eternal and universal love and mercy.

Leader: Searching after the purpose of life as a standard by which all else may be judged;
Desiring greatly to commune with Thee that we may know Thy will for us and for all men;
Praying that the spirit of Jesus Christ may pervade our own spirits.

People: We give unto Thee our spiritual selves which can be fed only by Thy Spirit, and strengthened only as we come unto Thee.

Leader: Desiring that our hands may be Thy hands, that our thoughts may be of whatever is true, honorable, just, pure, lovely, excellent, and worthy of praise;
Knowing that the greatest of all things is love; and that we must worship Thee in spirit and in truth.

People: We hereby dedicate ourselves in obedience to the commandment of Jesus Christ that "You shall love the Lord your God with all your heart, and with all your soul, and with all your strength, and with all your mind; and your neighbor as yourself."

BENEDICTION (in unison):

> May God be gracious unto us and bless us
>   and make his face to shine upon us,
> that thy way may be known upon earth,
>   thy saving power among all nations.
> Let the people praise thee, O God;
>   let all the people praise thee!
> In the matchless name of Christ we pray, Amen.

— An adaptation

POSTLUDE

AN INSTALLATION SERVICE FOR A YOUTH GROUP

Place a small table in the center of the room and arrange the chairs in a circle around it. The retiring officers are seated on one side, and the incoming officers on the other. Lighted candles are placed on the table and a candle is placed in the hand of each retiring and incoming officer.

HYMN: "Walk in the Light" — Manoah

Ritual of Light

13

(During the singing of the first stanza, the retiring president
lights the candle of the vice president, who in turn lights
the candle of the secretary. This continues from one officer
to another until all candles held by retiring officers are
lighted.)

SCRIPTURE READING: The Parable of the Talents — Matthew
25:14-30

LEADER: To each of us has been given something worthwhile
to do. The decision is with each of us. Shall I put forth my best
effort for the good of all concerned, or shall I let my opportunity
perish?

PRAYER (in unison):   Lord, may we recognize opportunities as
they come and do our best to make good in things worthwhile.
Keep us fit mentally, socially, physically and spiritually, that our
talents may be fully used in service to thee. In the name of the
Master Workman of the race, we pray.   Amen.

Ritual of Installation (conducted by the group sponsor)

SPONSOR: These lights burning brightly reflect the radiance of
many talents we possess. Through accepting and discharging
responsibility you have grown in trustworthiness. As we give light
from our candles to the newly elected officers we pray that you
may shed your light into the hearts and lives of others. Keep your
lights of Christian influence burning steadily for many will turn
to you for guidance along the way.

(Each retiring officer speaks briefly in turn, lights the
candle of his successor then exchanges places with him.
These brief statements will point the way to individual
initiative in line with the ideals and work of the office
indicated.)

PRESIDENT: To be chosen president of this group means that
you are set apart as one to whom all other members of the group
will look for ideals, standards, progress. Consider your office and
give to it your best in thought, word and deed.

NEW PRESIDENT: In accepting this office I agree to serve to
the limit of my ability.

VICE-PRESIDENT

NEW VICE-PRESIDENT

SECRETARY

NEW SECRETARY

TREASURER

NEW TREASURER

CHAIRMEN OF THE VARIOUS COMMITTEES

14

INCOMING CHAIRMEN OF THE COMMITTEES

This procedure will be followed through the entire list of officers. The statements to be made will be in keeping with the duties revealed in the constitution of the organization.

A WORD FROM THE NEW PRESIDENT

A CHARGE TO THE NEW OFFICERS: (by minister or some other mature person)

You have accepted these officers in leadership of this group of young people with all their meaning, responsibilities, privileges and opportunities for growth. Each office is an honor and far more.

By consistent personal effort, initiative and a cooperative spirit you will lead on to greater things — the true, the beautiful, the good.

Each member of the group you will serve has talent, ideals, purpose, and capacity for growth. These resources are now under your guidance.

We are deeply indebted to those who founded this organization and to those who have maintained its work and service. Each of you will strive to hold high the torch of leadership toward further victorious achievement. "Press forward, he conquers who will."

PRAYER

CLOSING HYMN: "Just As I Am, Thine Own to Be," or "Just As I Am"

— Selected

A CANDLELIGHT COMMISSIONING SERVICE

(Quiet music on the organ or a piano solo with violin obligato. A tall slender white lighted candle is placed on the altar or communion table. The leader takes his place at front.)

LEADER: In the beginning darkness covered the earth. Then God in his good time, sent his Son, Jesus Christ, to be the Light of the World. With his coming God lighted in the world a great Light, and wherever that light has shown, there mankind has found the more abundant life.

Jesus said, "God is light and in him there is no darkness. I am the Light of the World. Whoever follows me will never walk in darkness, but will have the light of life. You are the light of the world. So, your light is to shine before men that they may see the good you do and glorify your Father in heaven. I have set you to be a light for the Gentiles, to bring salvation to the end

15

of the earth. To open their eyes and turn them from darkness to light."

Today there is brought into the darkness this beautiful light, symbolic of the light which was Christ. He gave this light to his disciples, entrusting it to their care, commissioning them to carry it throughout the earth. Through the centuries it has been faithfully carried and passed from one hand to another until today it is handed on to you who have been chosen as leaders of your group. Just as surely as Christ depended upon his disciples to carry the light, so he is depending upon you and me to carry it forward wherever we may go in our own particular field of Christian activity and service — as a direct trust from him.

(As the elected officers' names are called they present themselves at the front facing the altar or table.)

LEADER: You have been singled out by the members of .... for special leadership. Your abilities have been recognized, and you have been chosen to minister through this talent. Sacred duties have been placed upon you. You have been elected to leadership by your associates and will be called upon so to live the high ideals of the Christ that others, seeing your good works, may wish to follow in your steps. It is well, as you begin this significant service that you should formally recognize your obligations and agree to fulfill them.

I ask you, do you heartily accept the office to which you have been called, and do you promise to faithfully fulfill the duties pertaining thereto?

OFFICERS (in unison): Yes, by the help of God.

LEADER: Receive then your light from the great central light, symbolic of Jesus Christ himself. May you keep the light burning brightly in the year ahead so that others may see and follow the light.

(Here each officer in turn goes to the altar or table, slowly and with dignity lights his own candle from the central light, then returns to his position, facing the altar.)

LEADER: Heroic spirits down through the centuries have been taking the torch from those who have gone on before. The early Christians, the martyrs, the great reformers, the pioneer fathers who came to this country in search of religious freedom, modern preachers and teachers of God's word — all would say —

"We caught their fire and carried it only a little way beyond, but there are those who wait for it, we know — those who will carry it on to victory."

16

Go ye forth and even as you pass the light on to those assembled here, continue to pass it on through the year ahead to everyone with whom you come in contact.

(Officers turn and face the audience with lighted candles.)

LEADER: To you, O youth of the churches, we turn for help in passing on this great light. Even as Christ needed helpers in the beginning of his ministry among men, even so you and I are his chosen torch bearers today. Our talents and our abilities may differ, but we can all, officers and followers, follow the gleam, the great Beacon Light, Jesus the Light of the World.

(Officers will pass down the aisles and light candles of those sitting next to them. Officers will then return to the front facing the altar. During the lighting of the candles "Follow the Gleam" is played quietly. When officers have returned to their places all will sing "Follow the Gleam.")

PRAYER (by Leader)

BENEDICTION: Grace and peace be multiplied to you in the knowledge of God and of Jesus our Lord."

— II Peter 1:2

— Adapted

A DEDICATION SERVICE FOR A MEN'S GROUP

PRELUDE: "A Charge to Keep I Have"

OPENING WORD BY THE LEADER:
(Include in this statement the occasion, the need for dedication, the task ahead and the group to be dedicated.)

HYMN: "Rise Up, O Men of God"

INVOCATION

SCRIPTURE READING Isaiah 6:1-8; Psalm 27; Joshua 24:14, 15

PRAYER HYMN: "Have Thine Own Way"

A PERIOD OF SILENT PRAYER: (closed by the leader)
(Topics for prayer thought may be suggested during this period, if desired)

SPECIAL MUSIC: (solo, male quartet, other available number)

MESSAGE: "The Choice Is Yours" (some outstanding layman, if possible)

RESPONSE OF DEDICATION

Leader: In the name of the Master of men who bids us put

our shoulders to the wheel, and facing the challenge of a task worth while, strive diligently toward the highest and best.

Men: We accept the challenge of Christian leadership and will strive to achieve in the name of Christ.

Leader: Realizing that our talents, which are many, are given us in trust and are to be dedicated toward the making of a better world —

Men: We now accept the high calling of Christian service and with courage choose the better Way.

Leader: Knowing full well that every day brings new and heavy demands toward making this world a safe and sane place in which to live —

Men: We pledge our utmost effort in this community and in our beloved church toward greater heights in faith, loyalty, and honest effort beginning at this fleeting moment which is ours to use.

HYMN OF DEDICATION: "Living for Jesus"

BENEDICTION (in unison):

Now unto him who is able to do exceeding abundantly above all that we ask or think, according to the power that worketh in us, unto him be the glory in the church and in Christ Jesus unto all generations for ever and ever. Amen.

A SERVICE OF WORSHIP AND DEDICATION
FOR WOMEN

PRELUDE

A MOMENT OF THOUGHTFUL SILENCE (everyone to bow in prayer with eyes closed)

ASCRIPTION OF PRAISE (in unison):

"Blessed is he whom thou dost choose and bring near, to dwell in thy courts!

We shall be satisfied with the goodness of thy house, thy holy temple."

— Psalm 65:4

HYMN: "Spirit of God, Descend upon My Heart"

SCRIPTURE LESSON: I Corinthians 13 or Proverbs 31:19-31

PRAYER OF THANKSGIVING AND INTERCESSION

SOLO

OFFERING: Offertory: "Thou Didst Leave Thy Throne" — *Margaret*

18

ADDRESS: "Women, Channels of God's Grace" (Minister, or a Woman guest speaker)

LITANY OF DEDICATION:

Leader: For the inflowing of Thy divine love, which will make our lives ever the unveiling of Thyself; our experiences a revelation of Thy ways among the children of men; our minds sanctuaries of Thy lowly spirit which takes the common things of life and makes them beautiful because Thou hast written eternity upon them,

Women: We join in humble prayer and joyous thanksgiving.

Leader: That we may every day wisely use and generously share our unmerited blessings "that Thy way may be known upon the earth" and in so doing justify every noble heritage, every worthy trust and every gift of Thy love.

Women: We pledge to so grow in the grace and knowledge of our Lord and Saviour, Jesus Christ.

Leader: For the compelling desire in our hearts to identify ourselves with the Christian womanhood of the world whose sensitive heart of love and concern can reflect in our day and in our world the mind and spirit of Christ,

Women: We make our supplication to an ever-listening, patient Father God.

Leader: To become guardians of the home, who shall in all circumstances practice those virtues of love which understand, forgive; are patient, serene, and unselfish; so that our family-living may be rich in religious experience, equipping each member for all the demands of life,

Women: With the assurance of Thy help we give ourselves.

Leader: With consecration to these high purposes of our Christian faith, and confident that we may grow above the shallow, the unimportant, and the trivial to find for ourselves the significance, the sanctity and the nobility of life, to the glory of Christ and his Church,

Women: We dedicate God's greatest gift, our lives.

PRAYER OF PERSONAL DEDICATION: (Minister)

CLOSING HYMN OF CONSECRATION: "O Master, Let Me Walk with Thee" — *Maryton*

— Adapted

AN INSTALLATION SERVICE FOR A WOMEN'S GROUP
(COUNCIL FELLOWSHIP OR GUILD)

(Appropriate changes of wording would make this an acceptable service for the installation of officers in a men's group.)

AN INTRODUCTORY WORD: You have been called to share in the greatest work of the church. Yours is the high honor of leading women to a richer, fuller life through Christian service. No nobler task could be given you. With every high privilege there are corresponding obligations. It is especially so in your case.

To each of you is entrusted special duties. Your life, your words, your attitude may influence many. Your supreme duty is, through your leadership, to exalt Christ and thus to inspire those who follow your leadership and who give themselves to the service of God and their comrades. You are asked therefore to pledge your acceptance of these responsibilities.

TO THE OFFICERS: Do you accept this responsibility in earnestness and prayer? Do you affirm your purpose to lend a spirit of cooperation in every possible way; to be in your place of duty unless illness or other emergency prevents; to continually strive to grow in effectiveness through study and prayer; and, to live such a life that your influence will lead others to the service of Christ?

If you accept these obligations, please signify by saying, "I do."

ANSWER: "I do."

TO THE WOMEN OF THIS CHURCH: As the women of this church do you affirm your purpose to support these officers as they strive to carry on their Christian task; to give encouragement and help when called upon; and to add the strength of your prayers to make the Women's Council of this church one that will efficiently function in developing Christian fellowship at home and world outreach toward the fulfillment of your mission in service to the Kingdom of our Master Jesus Christ?

If this is your sincere desire please say, "I do."

ANSWER: "I do."

THE CHARGE: Officers and women of the Christian Women's Fellowship — you have accepted the responsibility of your offices and your positions as followers. You are charged, therefore, to keep in mind the challenge of the task to which you are committed.

I charge you to study. Show yourselves approved; workmen that have no cause for shame.

I charge you to pray. Pray without ceasing. Sit often at the feet of the Master, learn of him how to pray, how to live, how to lead.

I charge you to keep ever before you the ultimate goal of all your efforts, the uniting of women around the world in service for Christ. You are to inspire sacrificial service. You are to help bring in the Kingdom of God in its fullness, and to speed the day when God's will shall be done on earth as it is in heaven.

Let us pray.

PRAYER

— Adapted from a service used in the First Christian Church, Fort Worth, Texas, and other churches far and near. Change the wording to meet local nomenclature and needs.

A CHURCH LEADERSHIP RECOGNITION SERVICE

(No leadership ritual is included in this service, but primary emphasis is placed on the priceless personalities leading the way in all departments of church life.)

ORGAN PRELUDE
PROCESSIONAL HYMN: "Faith of Our Fathers"
CALL TO WORSHIP AND GLORIA PATRIA
THE SCRIPTURE LESSON
THE MORNING PRAYER AND CHORAL RESPONSE
HYMN: "The Church's One Foundation"
SOLO
THE COMMUNION HYMN: "Have Thine Own Way Lord"
THE LORD'S SUPPER
OFFERING AND OFFERTORY
THE DOXOLOGY
SERMON: "Enthusiastically Interested" (The Minister)
HYMN OF INVITATION AND CONSECRATION: "All Hail the Power of Jesus Name"
SILENT PRAYER AND BENEDICTION
POSTLUDE

(The entire leadership roster was printed in worship folder including — elders, deacons, deaconesses, also the church school staff by classes and departments, and the women's department. Just before the sermon the minister called the entire roll of leaders with appropriate remarks.)

— Selected

21

A SERVICE OF LEADERSHIP DEDICATION

(Chairman of Education Division presiding)

PRAYER OF THANKSGIVING: (Elder or teacher)

WORDS OF WELCOME AND STATEMENT OF PURPOSE

INTRODUCTION OF PERSONNEL BY DEPARTMENTS

HYMNS OF GOOD FELLOWSHIP: "For the Beauty of the Earth", "I Love Thy Kingdom, Lord", "Forward through the Ages"

SCRIPTURE READING: John 3:1-15 (by a woman)

A BRIEF TALK: "To Lead in a Day Like This" (By minister or visiting leader. Pack it full of inspiration and challenge)

HYMN OF CONFLICT AND COURAGE: "God of Grace and God of Glory" (standing)

A LITANY OF DEDICATION AND THANKSGIVING (led by minister of education, or superintendent)

Leader: For the sinless life of Jesus Christ, our example, the same yesterday, today and forever, our inspiration and our guide —

Group: We give thee thanks, our Father.

Leader: For the wisdom and lessons of righteousness taught by Jesus, the Master Teacher, and their power to change the lives of men —

Group: We give thee thanks, our Father.

Leader: For thy boundless love so fully expressed in the presence of Jesus among the children of men —

Group: We give thee thanks, our Father.

Leader: For the ever-living message of the Christian Gospel applied to the hearts and lives of all men everywhere —

Group: We give thee thanks, our Father.

Leader: For the power of Jesus Christ to call us to our best, toward the noblest purposes —

Group: We give thee thanks, our Father.

Leader: To thee, O God, source of all truth, by whom we have been endowed with the ability to think, to feel, and to do —

Group: We dedicate our minds, O God.

Leader: To thee, the lover of all men everywhere whose sympathy, compassion and understanding is poured out in channels of blessing —

Group: We dedicate our hearts, O God.

Leader: To the Christian enterprise, beginning here and ex-

22

tending throughout the earth, and to the acceptance of Christian responsibility —

Group: We rededicate our time, our talent, our treasure to thee through thy Son Jesus Christ.

PRAYER OF DEDICATION AND BENEDICTION

> (In some churches a Leadership Day is planned annually at which time all leaders in the life of the church are seated in the Sanctuary and the minister's message points up the opportunities, satisfactions and soul-growth of Christian leadership.)

A SERVICE OF RECOGNITION AND DEDICATION FOR CHURCH SCHOOL LEADERS

> (This order of service was used to good effect within the morning worship hour by the Hennepin Avenue Methodist Church, Minneapolis, Minnesota. On a separate sheet the entire Church School Staff was listed.)

MINISTER: From the beginning, the Christian Church has been a teaching church. Through Christian nurture under many forms it has prepared its children for church membership and for Christian living; it has developed its youth for enlarging responsibility; and it has refined and vitalized the faith and works of its men and women. In thus spanning the years of life, Christian education has balanced with knowledge the zeal of new converts; it has saved the Church from false doctrine, and has quickened its conscience to the crying needs of our social life. It is Christian teaching that has prepared ministers and missionaries to preach the Gospel, nurtured the spirit alongside public and private worship, and matured young people and adults for significant Christian life in family and church, neighborhood and world. To this high and indispensable service and as the heirs of this noble tradition, you have been called.

CHURCH SCHOOL STAFF: It is the purpose of the officers and teachers of the Church School of this church:

To keep ever alert to the needs of those who are served,

To strive for ability to do God's work well,

To cultivate patience and understanding of those who are committed to our care,

To remember always that we are all learners at the feet of our common Lord,

To seek no reward but the approval of Him Who is the great leader, and

To keep ever aware of the great goal of helping children to accept Jesus Christ as their Lord and Savior, and to commit themselves wholeheartedly to His purpose and will for the world.

CONGREGATION: It is our purpose as parents and members of this congregation:

To cooperate gratefully with all who instruct our youth,

To strengthen their hands by giving them the resources needed for good teaching,

To volunteer our services to this great institution, asking that God will use us toward the end of helping others to know Him, even as some have shared this knowledge with us in times past, and

To make our homes proving-grounds for the practice of Christian living.

PRAYER OF DEDICATION
The Lord's Prayer
Choral Response

A LEADERSHIP DEDICATION RITUAL

TO THE OFFICERS ELECT: It is recorded in the story of the early church that when the number of disciples multiplied and the duties of the leaders were increased and became diversified, the church called its members together and chose men of good report, full of the spirit and of wisdom, to assist in the ministry; and that the officers thus chosen were set apart, or dedicated, to perform the duties of their office.

In like manner this congregation has chosen these men, and their presence signifies their acceptance of these important offices.

THE OFFICERS' PLEDGE: Trusting in Jesus Christ, my Lord and Savior, for strength, I promise him and this church that I will be faithful to the extent of my ability, regular in attendance, whole-hearted in giving, open-minded in planning, and patient in seeking the solution of problems.

I will seek to set a worthy example in the promotion of Christian fellowship among the members of this congregation and do hereby consecrate myself anew to the extension of Christ's Kingdom in our city, in our home land, and throughout the world-wide field of Christian service.

THE OFFICERS' RESPONSE: "We do."

TO THE CHURCH MEMBERS: We the pastor and officers of this Church call upon you to give attention to the reading of your pledge.

CHURCH MEMBERS' PLEDGE: Having chosen these officers to guide us in the administration of Church affairs, we, its members, do now pledge our loyalty to our leaders as they endeavor to guide us in a constructive church program.

We acknowledge our duty and our privilege, and declare our purpose to share with them in hastening the coming of Christ's Kingdom.

To this end we cheerfully and whole-heartedly seek to build up our church, and to lead men and women, youth and children, to choose Christ's way of life.

CHURCH MEMBERS' RESPONSE: "We do."

— Adapted

A CHARGE TO A YOUNG MINISTER
(On the Occasion of His Ordination)

Brother _____, you have found in your heart the desire to devote your life to the preaching of the Gospel of Christ; you have spent valuable time in preparation, that the work might be worthily done; you have won the confidence of your teachers, and the approval of those leaders who have known you in the church from your childhood. You come now, after mature deliberation and preparation to this final and ultimate committal of your life to this high purpose.

In behalf of the leaders, and of the churches whom they serve, I charge you, as Paul also charged Timothy of old, "Preach the Word." Your own wisdom is not sufficient. Your intelligence, your training, your continued and arduous study, you will need always and increasingly, but the ultimate message which you must build into the lives of men and the community must be larger than any wisdom of your own. No generation as much as ours, has proven the futility of mere human wisdom. I charge you, therefore, that by all diligence and by every means, you seek to ascertain the will and word of God, and translate it into the terms that men can grasp for daily living and for eternal measurements. Lean heavily on divine truth. "Preach the Word."

I charge you, "be an example unto believers in the Word, in daily living, in charity, in spirit, in faith, in purity." A minister has as many rights as any human but more responsibilities than most men. A true servant of Christ will waive rights to wield an influence for good. Your private life must be above reproach. What moral lapses in the lives of other men can be forgiven and forgotten, in a minister may be forgiven, but the memory of them may ruin his influence.

I charge you to remember the words of the Lord Jesus, how he said, "He that would lose his life for my sake shall find it," and "He that would be greatest among you, let him be servant of all." That eternal principle is as dependable as the law of gravitation. Its spirit in your soul will solve many problems that baffle human strength.

May the blessings of the Father God be upon you and lead you into the maximum utilization of your powers in the service of mankind, through the Savior of Man.

— Colby D. Hall

A CHARGE TO THE CONGREGATION ORDAINING A YOUNG MINISTER

Whatever a charge may mean in other contexts, in this situation it is interpreted to mean a challenge, and it is my happy task this evening to point up suggestions for this congregation's responsibility in relation to this man.

To this end, then, these suggestions:

You have chosen a servant;
    let him serve.
You have chosen a leader;
    let him lead.

You have chosen a man of GOD;
    help him remain so.

Guard his youth, and help him stay young
    all his life.
Let him hold to the idealism of youth,
    that with age it may neither mellow
    nor disintegrate.

Allow him to have new ideas
    and to spark them in your midst;
Do not be too anxious to quench these sparks
    with cold water.

Let differences which arise be marked
    by understanding
    and respect
    and humor
And bridged by your common purpose
    in serving God.

Lend him your encouragement
    and from time to time put it into words.
Do not allow the hour of sleep find him
    depressed or disheartened.

Allow him to draw his own conclusions
    about people and their problems,
As he may be able to see them in a different
    — and perhaps a better — light.

Allow him time for spiritual refreshment:
    quiet thinking
    and meditation
    and retreats for the growth of the spirit.

Don't let him feel the loneliness of the ministry,
But draw circles that will include
    him and his family,
And share with him and his wife
    genuine Christian love.

Have confidence in him, and through him,
    in the teachers who have taught him,
    in the minds of the great thinkers
        he has read,
    in the parents and family
        who have nurtured him,
    in GOD Who has chosen him for this part.

Tie him neither to the past
    nor to the post:
    Help him to know the best of what has been
        without insisting that he either
        uphold it or follow it if he
        knows a better way,
    Allow him opportunities to leave
        the immediate task from time to time
        so that he may look again on the
        total task of the Kingdom.

He has come to think of the Church as people;

May you always think of him as a person,
   and never as a machine
      or a divinity.
Keep in mind that you are ordaining him
   not to the ministry of this Church only,
   nor to the Brotherhood of the Disciples
      of Christ only,
   but to the Church Universal,
      stretching across the world in order
      to reach others who also wish
      to be in the Kingdom of GOD.

Pray for him;
Allow him to pray for you,
   recognizing that the latter
   may be more difficult for you
   than the former.

Remember that he represents among you not himself
   but the Christ of GOD;
Your response will be not to him,
   but to the Master of both of you.

He shall cultivate and prune and nourish,
   but you must bear fruit;
He shall plan and dream and pray,
   but you must carry plans and dreams and prayers
      to fulfillment.

Whose is the greater responsibility?
As great as is his,
   I venture to say it is the congregation's.
      But you are more than one,
      And you have among you GOD Himself,
         Who guides and strengthens and blesses.

Finally,
   Show by your practices and good deeds
      and lives of prayer
      your willingness to follow the One
         Whom he so willingly follows.

This will be his greatest reward . . .
   . . . and yours.

May GOD bless you both in this joint venture.

(Used by permission of William H. Martin, Associate Minister,
   All Peoples' Church, Los Angeles, California)

A SERVICE OF INSTALLATION AND DEDICATION OF A MINISTER

ORGAN PRELUDE

HYMN OF WORSHIP: "God of Our Fathers" (Stanzas 1 and 4)

CALL TO WORSHIP

Leader: Thanks be to God, who in Christ always leads us in triumph, and through us spreads the fragrance of the knowledge of Him everywhere.

Response: How beautiful upon the mountains are the feet of Him who brings good tidings.

Leader: Who publishes peace, who brings good tidings of good, who publishes salvation.

Response: O give thanks unto the Lord, Call upon His name, Make known His deeds among the people.

INVOCATION

SCRIPTURE READING: II Timothy 2:1-7

ANTHEM

SERMON: "The Measure of a Man" (Guest Minister)

COVENANT OF DEDICATION (Guest Leader)

Leader: In the name of the Lord Jesus Christ, and in His presence we are met here as a congregation to install _____ as pastor of the _____ Church. Inasmuch as this solemn act involves mutual obligations, I call upon you to unite in a covenant of dedication. Let the pastor to be installed stand, and make his declaration.

Pastor: Willingly do I reaffirm my ordination vows; Believing with all my heart that Jesus is the Christ, the Son of the Living God, and accepting the Holy Scriptures as inspired of God through the Holy Spirit, it is my sincere desire to devote my life to the ministry of the Word; so to live as to bring credit and not dishonor to the Gospel which I preach, and to fulfill to my utmost ability the office of a good minister of Jesus Christ. (Let the pastor be seated.)

Leader: Let the elders stand, and make their declaration.

Elders (In unison): We acknowledge the holy responsibilities of the office of the eldership to which we have been chosen; We affirm our love for this congregation whose oversight we have; And we offer ourselves in a common service with our pastor to serve the church of our Lord. (Let the elders be seated.)

Leader: Let the deacons and deaconesses stand, and make their declaration.

Deacons and Deaconesses: (In unison) We renew our pledge of loyalty to this church and to the office to which we have been appointed; and we promise to minister in all the material affairs of this congregation so as to maintain its reputation among all men. (Let the deacons and deaconesses be seated.)

Leader: (Will the members of the .... Church stand) Do you affirm your membership in Christ's church and your fellowship in this congregation with those who have obtained a like precious faith, renewing your vows of fidelity to our Lord Jesus Christ; do you solemnly covenant to work together with your pastor to extend the Gospel in its purity and power in this community and throughout the world, and as faithful servants of the Lord to give your pastor your utmost support in every way, according to your abilities and opportunities?

Congregation (in unison): We do.

Pastor: Brethren, standing with you, I reaffirm my willingness to be your pastor; and now covenant with you that in the strength and grace of our Lord Jesus Christ I will live a holy and circumspect life among you for an example, and will diligently and faithfully endeavor to perform all of the duties of a good minister of Jesus Christ on behalf of all the members of this congregation, and to the glory of His name and the edification of His Church.

PRAYER OF INSTALLATION (A Teacher or Elder)

WELCOME FROM THE CONGREGATION (Chairman of the Board)

GREETINGS FROM VARIOUS CIVIC AND MINISTERIAL ORGANIZATIONS

RESPONSE (The Candidate)

CLOSING HYMN: "Blest Be the Tie" (Stanzas 1 and 2)

BENEDICTION: And the peace of God, which passes all understanding, will keep your hearts and your minds in Christ Jesus. Amen.

POSTLUDE

(A reception for the new minister and guests immediately after the service.)

(It is wise to print the entire program and to list the persons participating.)

INSTALLATION OF A MINISTER OF MUSIC

(Careful examination of an order of worship used in a morning service revealed that out of twenty-eight items listed twenty-two called for the use of music. This is doubtless a typical proportion, and suggests why a number of the stronger churches are employing a minister of music who will be responsible not only for the regular and special music of the church, but also for the discovering, training and using of the musical talent and resources of the church. To assist such a church in the installation of the Minister of Music in a manner commensurate with this high calling, and to enhance this ministry in the thinking of the people, this order of worship has been prepared.)

PRELUDE: "If with All Your Heart"

ASCRIPTION OF PRAISE (Leader)

Make a joyful noise unto Jehovah, all the earth:
Break forth and sing for joy, yea, sing praises,
Sing praises unto Jehovah with the harp,
With the harp and the voice of melody,
With trumpets and sound of cornet
Make a joyful noise unto the King, Jehovah.
— Psalm 98:4-6

HYMN: "All Hail the Power of Jesus' Name" (Standing)

INVOCATION

SOLO

CALL TO PRAISE

Minister: O Lord open thou our lips:
Choir: *And our mouth shall show forth Thy praise.*
Minister: Praise ye the Lord:
Choir: *The Lord's name be praised. Amen.* (Traditional)

GLORIA PATRI (standing)

ANTHEM: "Send Out Thy Light"

CALL TO PRAYER

Minister: Unto Thee, O Jehovah, do we lift up our hearts:
People: *Yes, we lift up our hearts unto Thee, O Jehovah.*
Minister: Let us reverently bow in prayer.
Choir: *"Bless the Lord"*

PRAYER: (Minister)

RESPONSE: "Threefold Amen," by Choir or Instrument

A MESSAGE FROM THE PASTOR: "Music in the Life of Man"

A WORD FROM THE MINISTER OF MUSIC: "Releasing the Music That Is in Our Souls"

RITUAL OF INSTALLATION (all standing):

Minister: Today this church passes an important and very significant milestone in its history. We have called _____ to be the Minister of Music for this congregation and its constituency. Upon his shoulders will rest the responsibility of discovering, enlisting, training and guiding the musical talent of our church to the end that latent resources may be brought into active participation. This new venture should bring added privileges to all of us. As the minister of this church, I extend to him the hand of royal welcome. He may be assured of my full cooperation in this significant undertaking.

Choir: It shall be our earnest desire and supreme purpose to lend our talent and untiring assistance in making the worship, and the fellowship, of this church beautiful, attractive, and deeply spiritual by following the leadership of our new Minister of Music. We desire to share with him the responsibility of developing the musical resources of this church toward their most wholesome expression.

Congregation: You may depend on our assistance in the hymn singing. We will give cooperative attention to special music through which our Minister of Music and the Choir lead our worship. We will truly strive to express our devotion through the fine art of music as a part of our Christian privilege.

Minister of Music: This expression of royal welcome and interested cooperation should call forth my best endeavor to serve my Master faithfully as your Minister of Music. It challenges my best endeavor among the children, the young people and those older. It shall be my delight to help all age levels find their most appropriate expression of joy, goodwill, faith, thanksgiving, praise and love through music. To this end I now dedicate my life as one who serves, believing that the Christian religion is surcharged with the spirit of music, and finds its richest fruition through God-given talent dedicated to his praise and service. Together we will sing praises unto our God.

PRAYER OF CONSECRATION: (Minister or Elder)

CLOSING HYMN: "Lord Speak to Me"

BENEDICTION

Bind us together, O Lord, by all those aspirations which challenge us to a life of usefulness; by a consciousness of our kinship

with Thee. Strengthen us for the all but overwhelming tasks of
the Christian in this troubled world. Seeing in our fellows the
likeness of our Master, may we too become good servants of Jesus
Christ. So may the peace that passeth understanding rest and
abide with you now and forevermore. Amen.

— Robert W. Goodloe

A CHOIR DEDICATION SERVICE

PRELUDE

INTROIT

OPENING SENTENCE: Psalm 100:4, 5

PROCESSIONAL HYMN

CALL TO WORSHIP

Minister: It is a good thing to give thanks unto the Lord; and
to sing praises unto Thy Name, O Lord Most High; to show forth
Thy loving kindness in the morning, and Thy faithfulness every
night.

Congregation: I will praise Thee, O Lord, with my whole
heart. I will show forth Thy marvelous works. I will be glad and
rejoice in Thee. I will sing praises to Thy Name, O Thou Most
High.

THE LORD'S PRAYER

ANTHEM: "We Love Our Church, O God"

SCRIPTURE READING (Youth Director)

ANTHEM: "O God of Youth"

CHARGE TO THE CHORISTERS (Minister)

SERVICE OF DEDICATION

Minister: Will the members of the Carol Choir please stand.
You children, the like of whom Jesus took into His arms and
blessed, do you promise to learn well all that shall be taught you
in the Carol Choir? Do you promise?

Carol Choir: We do so promise.

Minister: Will the members of the Junior Choir please stand.
You who with eager hearts are learning to worship God, do you
promise to serve and sing for Him? Do you so promise?

Junior Choir: We do so promise.

Minister: Will the members of the Children's Choir please
stand. You who are giving your young lives in the service of
praise, do you promise to live for Jesus every day, and to be

faithful to Him by doing your best in the Children's Choir? Do you so promise?

Children's Choir: We do so promise.

Minister: Will the members of the Senior Choir please stand. You, who are seeking to discover the will of God in your lives and have committed yourselves through the choir to the ministry of your church, do you promise with the help of God, that you will keep your daily life in harmony with your music and fulfill to the best of your ability your duties as choristers in this church? Do you so promise?

Senior Choir: We do so promise.

LITANY OF DEDICATION

Minister of Music: To a conduct of life worthy of those who stand before others in public worship of God,

Choirs: We dedicate ourselves.

Minister of Music: To help in the fostering of reverence in the house of God, and to the creating of an atmosphere of worship,

Choirs: We dedicate ourselves.

Minister of Music: To lead the congregation in singing the praises of God, giving the honor due His name,

Choirs: We dedicate ourselves.

Minister of Music: To fill the house of worship with song and praise and prayer, and to help as we can in the lifting of the burdens of all who enter,

Choirs: We dedicate ourselves.

Minister of Music: To lead others by song into the Kingdom of God,

Choirs: We dedicate ourselves.

Minister of Music: To testify in glad and tuneful music our gratitude and love to Thee,

Choirs: We dedicate ourselves.

Minister of Music: Will you, the members of this congregation and parents of the choristers, recognize the devotion and the service of these choirs, receive them as your choirs and in so far as at all possible support them by your encouragement, and faithful attendance at the worship services of this church? Do you so promise?

Congregation: We do so promise.

HYMN OF DEDICATION

RECESSION OF THE CHOIRS

BENEDICTION

— Adapted

SUGGESTIONS POINTING THE WAY TOWARD
DEDICATION OF PERSONS

Every honorable calling, vocation, or profession offers opportunity for public recognition and dedication at a strategic time in a local church or community. We give honor in this way to priceless personalities, well-known and loved among their fellows.

Church leaders, aware of these high points of human interest, may very appropriately provide a recognition or dedication ritual to lift into the highest level of thinking, speaking and acting the sterling character qualities of those to be honored. Time and heart-power expended in arranging for such recognition is indeed valuable.

In seeking to live life at its best and to give public recognition to worthy achievement, alert leadership will provide for these special occasions. Here are a few of the many fields of leadership from which well-known names may be chosen —

A dedicated statesman
A dedicated minister
A dedicated minister of Christian Education
A dedicated minister's wife
A dedicated teacher
A dedicated mother
A dedicated father
A dedicated lawyer
A dedicated artist
A dedicated architect
A dedicated business man
A dedicated physician or surgeon, or nurse
A dedicated secretary

(Many others might be added)

PART II

DEDICATION OF PLACES

DEDICATION OF CHURCH BUILDING SITE

(IN THE SANCTUARY)

PRELUDE
CHORAL INTROIT: "O Worship the Lord"
HYMN OF FAITH: "The Church's One Foundation"
OPENING SENTENCES
    Minister: The Lord be with you,
    People: And with thy spirit.
    Minister: Let us pray.
INVOCATION (The minister)
RESPONSE BY THE CHOIR: "The Lord Is in His Holy Temple"
SILENT ROLL CALL: (In silence we recall the names of our comrades who have in days gone by worshipped with us here)
SCRIPTURE READING: From Jeremiah 31; Isaiah 61; Ezekiel 11; Acts 2
GLORIA PATRI
ANTHEM
THE MORNING OFFERING
    Sentence of Scripture
    Offering received
    Doxology and Prayer of Dedication
THE COMMUNION OF THE LORD'S SUPPER
PROCESSIONAL: "Lead On, O King Eternal"
    (At this point the congregation is adjourned and all move in cars to the new church site. Ushers will dismiss the congregation in some orderly procedure.)

(AT THE NEW SITE)

OPENING CEREMONY: Psalm 1
PASTORAL PRAYER AND THE LORD'S PRAYER
GREETINGS (Representatives from the city, county, and state church organizations.)
LITANY OF DEDICATION (Leader, a Layman)
    Leader: Surely the Lord is in this place and I knew it not; this is none other but the house of God, and this is the gate of heaven. Brethren, we are met in this most memorable place to

set apart these lands and ourselves to the holy task of building a church. Today we consecrate this ground to God's service and seek his guidance as we do so. Let us pray.

PRAYER OF INVOCATION (A Layman)

Leader: For this beautiful place with its promise of praise and service to Thee, our Father —

People: We lift our voices in gratitude and praise.

Leader: For the richness of the years in which our family of faith has been blessed and prospered, and for all who have shared ties of kinship and labors in thy Kingdom —

People: We thank Thee, our kind and loving Father.

Leader: In these present moments as our hearts seek future realization of a church for our children and for their children, we stand by faith and look with confidence to Thee in whose hands are all the issues of life —

People: Look within our hearts, O God, and discern our most secret motives. Judge us according to Thy perfect understanding and deliver us by Thy perfect love from ways of discouragement and despair.

Leader: As the earth is the Lord's and the fulness thereof, the world and they that dwell therein, so even this chosen place of sanctuary belongs to Thee, the Creator and the Sustainer of all abiding things, O God. Give us the grace of all good stewards who remember their Creator daily and who walk confidently in the light of Thy presence. Lay upon us all, our Father, the burden of cleansing this hallowed ground of any desecrating act or any unworthy gift as we build together —

People: All things come of Thee, O Lord, and of thine own have we given Thee.

Leader: We dedicate this place to the building of a worthy house of prayer,

People: Teach us, our Father, how to pray.

Leader: We dedicate this ground to the mission of Christ's redemptive Church,

People: Send us forth to the task of redemption in Christ's name, O God.

Leader: We dedicate this land as an inheritance for all who belong to Thee and who call upon Thee in faith,

People: Grant us the right to inherit the riches of life eternal by Thy Grace, O Lord.

Leader: We dedicate this field to the sowing of the seed of Thy Word,

People: Do Thou bring forth bountiful harvest of righteous

lives and grant us the joy of sharing in the harvest, through Christ the living Word.

CEREMONY OF MEMORIALS

OFFERING TO THE NEW CHURCH

SPECIAL MUSIC

PRAYER OF DEDICATION AND BENEDICTION

> (The above is an adaptation from the Oak Cliff Christian Church, Dallas, Texas. Hugh M. Riley, minister at the time.)

A GROUND BREAKING SERVICE

CALL TO WORSHIP (Minister of Education)

THE DOXOLOGY (Congregation)

THE INVOCATION (Chairman of the Church Board)

SCRIPTURE READING: I Chronicles 29:10-16 (Building Committee Chairman)

ADDRESS (Guest Minister)

LITANY OF DEDICATION

Leader: Beloved in the Lord, we rejoice that God has put into the hearts of his people to break this ground to the glory of his name. I now set it apart for the building of the Church. Let us, therefore, as we are assembled, solemnly dedicate this site to its proper and sacred uses —

To the glory of God, the Father, who
  has called us by his grace;
To the honor of his Son, who loved us
  and gave himself for us;
To the power of the Holy Spirit, who
  illuminates and sanctifies us,
People: We break this ground.

Leader: For the worship of God in prayer and praise; for the preaching of the everlasting Gospel; for the celebration of the Lord's Supper,
People: We break this ground.

Leader: For the comfort of all who mourn; for strength for those who are tempted; for light for those who seek the Way,
People: We break this ground.

Leader: For the hallowing of family life; for teaching and guiding the young; for the administration of Christian baptism to those who believe,

41

People: We break this ground.

Leader: For the conversion of sinners; for the promotion of righteousness; for the world outreach program of the Church,

People: We break this ground.

Leader: In the unity of the faith; in the bond of Christian Brotherhood; in charity and good will toward all men everywhere,

People: We break this ground.

Leader: In gratitude for the labors of all who love and serve this church; in loving remembrance of those who have finished their earthly course; in the hope of a blessed immortality through Jesus Christ our Lord,

People: We break this ground.

Leader and People: We now, the people and congregation, compassed about with a great cloud of witnesses, grateful for our heritage, aware of the sacrifices of our fathers in the faith — confessing that apart from us their work cannot be perfected, do dedicate ourselves anew to the worship and service of Almighty God, through Jesus Christ our Redeemer.   Amen

ACT OF GROUND-BREAKING (Church School superintendent presiding)

> (As the name of each department representative is called that person will take a spade in hand and stand in the line outlining the ground floor of the building. When all representatives are in the line a signal is given for all to turn a portion of the earth at the same time.)

Church School Representatives
Church Group Representatives
Professional Representatives
   The Architect
   The Building Contractor

HYMN OF DEDICATION: "The Church's One Foundation"
BENEDICTION   (A Guest Minister)

> Adapted from First Christian Church, Midland, Texas

A CORNERSTONE LAYING SERVICE

INTRODUCTORY REMARKS

HYMN: "America" (All singing, led by Trombonist, or Cornetist)

RESPONSIVE SCRIPTURE READING: (Led by Guest Minister)

Leader:
>   Remember, O Lord, in David's favor,

all the hardships he endured;
how he swore to the Lord
and vowed to the almighty one of Jacob.

Congregation:
I will not enter my house
or get into my bed;
I will not give sleep to my eyes
or slumber to my eyelids,
until I find a place for the Lord
A dwelling place for the Mighty
One of Jacob.

Leader:
Let us go to his dwelling place,
Let us worship at his footstool.

Congregation:
Arise, O Lord, and go to thy resting place,
thou and the ark of thy might.

Leader:
Let the priests be clothed with righteousness,
and let thy saints shout for joy.

Congregation:
For thy servant David's sake
Do not turn away the face of thy anointed One.

PRAYER   (A Guest Minister)

HYMN

SCRIPTURE LESSON: I Corinthians 3:9-17 (A Guest Minister)

ADDRESS: "The Chief Corner Stone" (A Guest Minister)

OFFERING FOR THE BUILDING FUND   (Chairman of the Building Committee)

CORNER STONE LAYING (Chairman of the Board, assisted by the Architect)

DEPOSITS IN THE CORNER STONE CHEST
(Each person will bring his particular contribution, tell what it is he is placing in the chest, place it and retire.)

PRAYER OF DEDICATION: (An Elder)

SEALING OF THE CORNER STONE: (The Builder)

CHOIR

MEDITATION   (The Minister)

BENEDICTION
Now unto him that is able to keep us from falling and to present us faultless before the presence of his glory with

exceeding joy, to the only wise God, our Savior, be glory, and majesty, dominion and power, both now and ever. Amen.

— Jude 24, 25

(An adaptation combining the Overland Park Christian Church, Missouri and First Christian Church, Lufkin, Texas)

DEDICATION OF AN EDUCATIONAL BUILDING

PRELUDE

CALL TO WORSHIP

> This is the day which the Lord has made;
> let us rejoice and be glad in it,
> O give thanks to the Lord for he is good;
> for his steadfast love endures forever.
>
> — Psalm 118:24-29

INVOCATION

HYMN OF PRAISE: "I Love to Tell the Story"

RESPONSIVE READING: Psalm 1; John 15:1-11

SOLO: "O, Lord Most Holy"

PRAYER

OFFERTORY

DOXOLOGY

PRESENTATION OF THE SPEAKER

HYMN OF ASSURANCE: "How Firm a Foundation" (Stanzas 1, 2, 5)

DEDICATORY MESSAGE: (Guest Minister or Educator)

THE LITANY OF DEDICATION

Minister: In recognition of the Great Commission which bids us "Go — make disciples — baptize — teach," and in harmony with the message which reads that "Jesus advanced in wisdom, in stature, and in favor with God and man" we come to this moment of dedication praying that blessings in over-flowing abundance may prevail in the hearts of all who have made this happy moment possible.

To the sowing of the good seed of the Kingdom in the hearts of all of our people, young and old,

People: We dedicate our Education Building to the ministry of teaching.

44

Minister: To the purpose of developing a school where the Holy Scriptures may be read, interpreted, and known,

People: We dedicate our Education Building.

Minister: For the spiritual enrichment of life as it unfolds through childhood,

People: We dedicate our building.

Minister: For the nurture of youth and the enrichment of the home,

People: We dedicate our building.

Minister: To provide an appointed place where the soul of man may quest for the Good, the Beautiful and the True,

People: We dedicate our building.

Minister: To make accessible an atmosphere where the art of worship may be rehearsed and learned,

People: We dedicate our building.

Minister: For the training of life in the Christian Way, that character may reflect the life of the Master,

People: We dedicate our building.

Minister: To maintain a school of intelligent faith, wherein we may learn to give a reason for the faith that is in us,

People: We dedicate our building.

Minister: For the enrichment of social and recreational life through fellowship with those who share in the mind of Christ,

People: We dedicate our Education and Fellowship Building.

Minister and People: We now, the people of this church and congregation, compassed about with a great cloud of witnesses, remembering the sacrifices of the fathers, upon whose foundations we are building, dedicate ourselves anew to the teaching of the word of God in both precept and example.

Bless the Lord, O my soul;

And all that is within me, bless His holy name. Amen.

PRAYER OF DEDICATION

BENEDICTION

POSTLUDE: "A Mighty Fortress Is Our God"

SERVICE FOR AN ANNIVERSARY OF THE DEDICATION OF A CHURCH BUILDING

PRELUDE

CALL TO WORSHIP   (in unison)

Surely I come not into the tabernacle

Nor go up into my bed;
I will not give sleep to mine eyes,
Or slumber in my eyelids;
Until I find out a place for the Lord,
A tabernacle for the mighty God of Jacob.

— David

HYMN

INVOCATION AND THE LORD'S PRAYER

COMMUNION SERVICE

Hymn

The Lord's Supper

Hymn

OFFERING SERVICE

Sentence of Scripture

The Offering

Doxology (standing)

SCRIPTURE READING

AN AFFIRMATION OF OUR FAITH   (in unison):

God is spirit; and they that worship Him must worship Him in spirit and in truth.

God is light; and if we walk in the light, as He is in the light, we have fellowship with one another.

God is love; and everyone that loveth is born of God and knoweth God.

Jesus is the Son of God; and God hath given to us eternal life, and this life is in His Son.

We are the children of God; and He has given us of His Spirit.

If we confess our sins He is faithful and just to forgive us our sins, and to cleanse us from all unrighteousness.

The world passeth away and the lust thereof but he that doeth the will of God abideth forever.

(From the Gospel of John)

PRAYER HYMN

THE MORNING PRAYER

A MESSAGE IN SONG

SERMON: "Except the Lord Build the House"

HYMN OF INVITATION

A RESPONSE OF REDEDICATION

Minister: In the spirit of gratitude to our heavenly Father by whose favor, inspiration and guidance we have come to this Fortieth Anniversary of the Dedication of this building.

46

Congregation: We re-dedicate this house of worship.

Minister: In love for our beloved church and in reverent memory of all those who by their service and sacrifice down through the years have bequeathed to us this valuable church property.

Congregation: We re-dedicate this house of worship.

Minister: In grateful appreciation of the generosity of the members and friends of this church, the spirit of unity, and of loyalty prevailing throughout the whole church.

Congregation: We re-dedicate this house of worship today and re-consecrate our lives to the service of Christ our Lord, and to the world-wide extension of his Kingdom.

BENEDICTION

THREEFOLD AMEN: (Piano or Organ)

POSTLUDE

DEDICATION OF A CHURCH SANCTUARY

PRELUDE

PROCESSIONAL HYMN: "O God, Our Help in Ages Past"

CALL TO WORSHIP

THE LORD'S PRAYER

RESPONSE

ANTHEM

SERMON

INVITATION HYMN: "I Love Thy Kingdom Lord"

OFFERTORY

DOXOLOGY

OFFERTORY PRAYER

DEDICATORY LITANY

Minister: That we behold the beauty of the Lord and inquire in His holy temple

Congregation: We dedicate this church and consecrate our lives.

Minister: That an altar may here be raised, where men may seek after God if haply they might find Him

Congregation: We dedicate this church and consecrate our lives.

47

Minister: That peace and good will may grow between nations and classes

Congregation: We dedicate this church and consecrate our lives.

Minister: That the gospel of the Lord Jesus Christ may be taught and practiced throughout the world

Congregation: We dedicate this church and consecrate our lives.

Minister: That the equality of all Christians before God may here be recognized

Congregation: We dedicate this church and consecrate our lives.

Minister: That the spirit of Jesus may control all human relationships and hallow all personalities

Congregation: We dedicate this church and consecrate our lives.

Congregation: (all joining) "O Almighty and everlasting God, Thou dwellest not in temples made with hands, neither art Thou worshipped with men's hands, as though Thou needest anything, seeing that Thou givest to all life and breath and all things; when we bring Thee our best, we serve Thee only with what is Thine own; and when we have done all, we are but unprofitable servants. Yet, do Thou, O Lord, who delightest Thyself in the praises of the Sanctuary, accept the offering of this house which Thy people have builded to the glory of Thy holy name. We consecrate it to Thee, the Father, the Son, and the Holy Ghost, to be henceforth the House of God, and a gate to heaven; we set it apart from all common and worldly uses, for a temple and a sanctuary, where Thy holy Gospel shall be preached; where the prayers of the Church shall be made unto Thee without ceasing; where Thy high praises shall be devoutly sung; where the ordinances of Thy Word shall be duly administered; to which Thy people shall throng with cheerful steps. Let the glory of the Lord fill this house, and the spirit of God descend and dwell in His Church. Amen.

COMMUNION SERVICE

RECESSIONAL HYMN: "Glorious Things of Thee Are Spoken"

BENEDICTION (Minister)

ORGAN POSTLUDE (Organist-Director)

Adapted from Dedication Service of the Park Avenue Christian Church, New York City

48

DEDICATION OF A NEW ADDITION
TO A CHURCH PLANT

ORGAN PRELUDE

PROCESSIONAL HYMN: "The Church's One Foundation"

INVOCATION AND THE LORD'S PRAYER

GLORIA

GREETINGS FROM PARTICIPATING PERSONNEL

HYMN: "All Hail the Power of Jesus Name"

SCRIPTURE READING: I Corinthians 12:12-27

ANTHEM

OFFERTORY

DEDICATION OF GIFTS

SOLO

SERMON: "How Big Is Your Church?"

LITANY OF DEDICATION

Minister: Forasmuch as it pleased Almighty God to put it into the hearts of his servants to add to and improve this house which years ago as a new building was dedicated to God, let us now fulfill the high purpose for which we are assembled, that of dedicating to the honor of God and his Kingdom the new addition and improvements to this house of God. (Let us pray)

Minister: Our heavenly Father, who hast so graciously led in this project and so abundantly blessed each step of the way,

Congregation: We offer our thanks to Thee.

Minister: For the gifts of Thy people which have made possible the addition to this building and the improvements within the building, and for the skilled workmanship that has entered into all these,

Congregation: We offer our thanks to Thee.

Minister: For the opportunities that lie before us, with more adequate facilities, to serve Thee by serving Thy children,

Congregation: We offer our thanks to Thee.

Minister: We take now that which we have built, and in acknowledgment of Thy goodness,

Congregation: We dedicate the addition and all the improvements to Thee and to Thy service.

Minister: For the teaching of Thy Word and the training of children and youth in Christian faith and life,

Congregation: We dedicate this Christian Education Building to Thee.

Minister and Congregation: In the name of the Father and of the Son and of the Holy Spirit, Amen.

DOXOLOGY

BENEDICTION: II Corinthians 13:14

ORGAN POSTLUDE

South Park Presbyterian Church, Rock Island, Illinois

DEDICATION OF A HOUSE OF WORSHIP

ORGAN PRELUDE

CALL TO WORSHIP

PROCESSIONAL HYMN: "The Church's One Foundation"

INVOCATION: Minister

CHOIR RESPONSE

THE SIGNIFICANCE OF THIS SERVICE (Chairman of the Building Council)

RECOGNITION OF CITY, DENOMINATIONAL, AND ORGANIZATIONAL REPRESENTATIVES

WORDS OF GREETING

OFFERTORY

Hymn: "We've a Story to Tell to the Nations"
Offering Received
Doxology and Prayer of Dedication

ANTHEM

DEDICATORY MESSAGE (Guest Minister)

SOLO

LITANY OF DEDICATION

Pastor: Having been led by the good hand of God, and enabled by His grace and power to complete this house of worship, we now stand in His holy presence and dedicate this building to Him.

People: "Bless the Lord, O my soul, and forget not all his benefits." "Bless His holy name forever."

Pastor: To the glory of God the Father, who has called us by His grace; to the honor of His Son, who loved us, and gave Himself for us; to the praise of the Holy Spirit, who illumines and sanctifies us;

People: We dedicate this house.

Pastor: For the worship of God in prayer and praise; for the preaching of the everlasting gospel of Jesus Christ; for the observance of the New Testament ordinances of Baptism and the Lord's Supper;

People: We dedicate this house.

Pastor: For the dedication of our children; for their nurture in the instruction of the Lord;

People: We dedicate this house.

Pastor: For the Christian education of our youth; For their salvation by faith in Jesus Christ; For their enlistment in the causes of His Kingdom;

People: We dedicate this house.

Pastor: For the comfort of all who mourn; for the strength of those who are tempted and tested; for the light of those who seek the way;

People: We dedicate this house.

Pastor: For the building of Christian homes; for the promotion of personal and social righteousness in our community, for the extension of the Kingdom of God to the ends of the earth;

People: We dedicate this house.

Pastor: In grateful recognition of the noble leadership of former pastors and the faithful labors of former members; in affectionate remembrance of our beloved dead whose prayers and gifts are joined with ours today;

People: We dedicate this house and rededicate ourselves to God in the name of Jesus Christ. Amen.

RECESSIONAL HYMN: "Faith of Our Fathers"

BENEDICTION

CHURCH CHOIR RESPONSE — Sevenfold Amen — Stainer

ORGAN POSTLUDE: "Now Thank We All Our God" — Kaufmann

As used by the First Baptist Church, Moline, Illinois

DEDICATION OF A CHURCH CAMP

CALL TO WORSHIP

> Come, let us go up to the mountain of the Lord,
>   To the house of the God of Jacob;
> that he may teach us his ways
>   and that we may walk in his paths.
>   — Isaiah 2:3

INVOCATION   (A Minister)

HYMN OF NATURE: "For the Beauty of the Earth" (Stanzas 1, 2)

SCRIPTURE READING: Psalm 19:1-6   (A Youth Representative)

MESSAGE OF DEDICATION: "Our Hearts Rejoice"

LITANY OF DEDICATION

Leader: For the beauty of Thy universe as it reveals the wonder and beauty of Thy being and Thy concern and love for man,

Group: We thank Thee, O Lord.

Leader: For this camp where, in the glory and majesty of nature, we may come apart to be renewed and strengthened,

Group: We thank Thee, O Lord.

Leader: For the youth and adults whose lives will take on new meaning and clarity as they study and work here, in order to witness more fully to the supreme love shone in the gift of Thy Son,

Group: We thank Thee, O Lord.

Leader: For the counselors and leaders whose dedicated time and lives seek to relate those eternal truths of Thy being,

Group: We thank Thee, O Lord.

Leader: In order that the lives of dedicated leaders might shed the light of truth upon the pathways of life so that others might find direction for their lives,

Group: We dedicate this camp, O Father.

Leader: In order that youth may enjoy and appreciate the out-of-doors, and, in a community of seeking people, experience the reality of Christian love, and awareness of the immediate presence of God,

Group: We dedicate this camp, O Father.

Leader: In order that adults may seek Thee in the quiet and solitude of Thy creation,

Group: We dedicate this camp, O Father.

Leader: To the renewal of our spiritual life and witness to the message of Thy Son,

Group: We dedicate ourselves, O God.

Leader: To the work of Thy Church in the lives of youth and adults,

Group: We dedicate ourselves, O God. Amen.

PRAYER OF DEDICATION

Creator of life and light,
We bless thee this day for the beauty of thy world,

For sunshine and flowers, storm cloud and starry night,
For the first radiance of dawn and the last smoldering glow
  of the sunset.

We thank thee for physical joy,
For the ecstasy of swift motion,
For deep water to swim in,
For the goodly smell of rain on dry ground,
For hills to climb, and hard work to do,
For all skill of hand and eye,
For music that lifts our hearts in one breath to heaven,
For the handclasp of a friend,
For the gracious loveliness of children.

We thank thee, above all, for spiritual beauty and joy,
For home love, for mother love, for child love,
For the instant assent of our hearts
To the truth that is spoken by prophet or poet,
For the exceeding bliss of the touch of thy hand,
Awakening suddenly our drowsy souls
Into blessed awareness of thy presence with us and in us:
For all these thy sacraments of beauty and joy
We thank thee our Lord and our God.

Now may we dedicate this camp to thy service.
Guide its use as we seek through its ministry
To witness to those things which are ultimate.
In the spirit of fellowship and worship may
We use it to thy glory. Amen.

HYMN: "Forward Through the Ages"
> Forward through the ages, In unbroken line,
> Move the faithful spirits, At the call divine;
> Gifts in differing measure, Hearts of one accord,
> Manifold the service, One the sure reward.

> REFRAIN:

> Forward through the ages, In unbroken line,
> Move the faithful spirits, At the call divine. Amen.

RECOGNITIONS AND ANNOUNCEMENTS
BENEDICTION
> Let the words of my mouth, and the
>   meditation of my heart
> be acceptable in thy sight,
> O Lord, my rock and my redeemer.
> — Psalm 19:14

This service of dedication, prepared by a ministerial student was used in the dedication of Camp Fellowship, on Lake Fannin.

DEDICATION OF A BUSINESS ESTABLISHMENT

(The opening for such a dedication as this may grow out of a personal contact between a minister and one of his key churchmen who is opening a new business. A suggestion from the minister will serve to pave the way for this dedication.)

OPENING VERSES FROM THE BIBLE

What does the Lord your God require of you, but to fear the Lord your God, to walk in all his ways, to love him, to serve the Lord your God with all your heart and with all your soul and to keep the commandments and statutes of the Lord, which I command you this day for your good   (Deut. 10:12, 13).

INVOCATION

STATEMENT OF PURPOSE

Today we are met under these friendly surroundings in this newly established place of business to rededicate its owner and manager to God and to give religious recognition to this business concern.

It is altogether fitting and proper that a place of business should be established. Business acumen, thrift, diligence, honesty, are worthy traits of character. The owner, and manager of this business house possesses these traits of character. They are imbedded in a sound Christian faith. He is active in his church. We are here today as a group of his comrades and friends to point up the significance of this forward step he has taken. We marvel at what has been achieved. We rejoice in this privilege. We congratulate our friend, _____.

SCRIPTURE READING: Romans 8:31-39, or I Corinthians 3:10-16

SPECIAL MUSIC

A WORD OF COMMITMENT: (By the Owner and Manager of the Business Concern)

This is a day of rejoicing for me and for my family, and for those who are to be associated with us in this business enterprise. We feel that except the Lord build the house they labor in vain who build it.

It is our supreme purpose to do what is good, to do what the Lord requires, to deal justly with our customers, to render kindly dealings toward everyone with whom we have contact, and in deep humility to give God the glory. (We hereby commit at least one-tenth of our increase to the work of Christ's Church.)

LITANY OF DEDICATION

Minister: To the end that all who enter this place — of business will sense the true spirit of brotherhood and service,

Group: We dedicate this Business Concern.

Minister: Toward the continuing spirit of friendliness, honest dealings, satisfactory service, noble business enterprise,

Group: We dedicate this Business Concern and the entire personnel managing, helping, serving here; seeking to make a living in this community while keeping their own lives above reproach.

PRAYER OF BLESSING AND BENEDICTION

DEDICATION OF A HOME

(There is an increasing demand for home dedication rites and ceremonies. Such a dedication could be arranged at Christmas time, during National Family Week in May, or at any other strategic time, particularly on the completion of a new home or parsonage. When a newly married couple establishes a home in a house of their own, it would be an excellent time for such a service of dedication.)

AN INTRODUCTORY STATEMENT   (The Minister)

The home is still God's first and holiest school. Jesus was born in Bethlehem of Judea. He shared in the life of three homes during the few short years he spent in the flesh among men. His first home was in the village of Nazareth where his childhood and youth were spent. Then, when rejected in Nazareth, during the early days of his ministry, the family moved to Capernaum where he made headquarters during much of his ministry. The third home was with his three close friends — Mary, Martha and Lazarus — at Bethany near Jerusalem. Today he seeks to share in your home and mine.

READING OF SCRIPTURE   (From the Family Bible):

The Home Circle in Bible Times —

1. Ruth and Naomi, Ruth 1:1-18
2. Mary and Martha, Luke 10:38-42

HYMN

PRAYER   (By a Home-Maker)

Make this home a Bethany, O Father. Sit with us at the table. Draw us from our worldly cares as our Savior drew Martha in the days of long ago. Be our life, as Jesus was the life of Lazarus. Show us the better part as day by day we share home life with those we love. Grant thy special blessing upon this home today. In the name of the Christ of Galilee we pray. Amen.

CEREMONY OF LIGHT AND FIRE

(While one lights candles, symbols of home cheer, someone says:)

There are many lights of home, but love
that goes from heart to heart is the
brightest of them all.

(After the candles have been lighted, someone continues:)

Love is an incense from an altar bright
Where candles shine with clear and mellow light;
It is a lamp that cheers us when we roam,
And a kindly spark that lights the fires of home.

(If there is a fireplace let the husband put on kindling and light the fire, as the wife reads:)

"Kneel always when you light a fire
Kneel reverently
To God for his unfailing charity."

— John Oxenham

A TOUCH OF BEAUTY

(Unveiling of pictures, tapestries, or heirlooms, with brief mention)

ACT OF DEDICATION

Husband: We humbly dedicate this house with sincere appreciation toward its builders, and with deep gratitude for God's leading in bringing us here to make a home.

Wife: We dedicate the doors of our home to hospitality and security.

Husband: We dedicate the windows that our home may be lighted and cheerful, that we may look out on others with kindness and neighborliness.

Wife: We dedicate our furniture and all other home equipment with thoughts of consideration for all whose labors and skill add to our comfort.

Husband: We dedicate our books in which our friends through the printed page contribute much to our edification and enjoyment.

Wife: We dedicate our pictures and tapestries as symbols of beauty and attractiveness, hallowed memory and thoughtfulness.

Husband: We dedicate this home to love and wholesome companionship, to courage and patience, to courtesy and mutual understanding, to loyalty and human dignity.

Wife: We dedicate this home to work and leisure, to serious thinking and the gaiety of laughter; to music and restful relaxation.

Husband: We dedicate the life of this home to service of God and our fellow-men, a unit of God's Kingdom on earth, in which we are privileged to live worthily, and to be fitted to cross the threshold into life eternal. When we come to the river of death may we be aware that our Father owns the land on both sides.

PRAYER OF DEDICATION (The Minister)

MUSIC (Both Instrumental and Vocal in Good Fellowship)

CLOSING PRAYER (everyone participating):

> May God be gracious to us and bless us
> and make his face to shine upon us,
> that thy way may be known upon earth,
> Thy saving power among all nations.
> Let the people praise thee, O God;
> Let all the people praise thee.
>
> — Psalm 67:1-3

SERVICE FOR A MORTGAGE BURNING
(Chairman of the Church Board presiding)

PRELUDE

INTRODUCTORY SENTENCES (Minister)

> Our feet are standing within thy gates, O Jerusalem.
> I was glad when they said unto me,
> Let us go unto the house of the Lord.
> Jerusalem, thou are builded as a city that is compact together;
> Whither the tribes go up, even the tribes of the Lord,
> To give thanks unto the name of the Lord.
>
> — From Psalm 122

Today is not yesterday, we ourselves change; how can our works and thoughts, if they are always to be the fittest, continue always the same? Change, indeed, is painful, yet ever needful; and if memory has its force and worth so also has hope.

> — Thomas Carlyle

HYMN OF PRAISE: "Come, Thou Almighty King"

INVOCATION   (Minister)

BRIEF HISTORY OF THE CONGREGATION AND ITS BUILD-
ING   (Church Board Chairman)
> (Include here the date of organization, first building,
> present building, personnel)

SCRIPTURE READING: God's House — Selections from Matthew 21 and Luke 4   (Minister)

SPECIAL MUSIC

KINDLING THE FIRE
> Leader: In the spirit of gratitude to our heavenly Father by
> whose favor, inspiration and guidance we have been able to free
> our church home from all indebtedness;
> People: We burn this mortgage.
> Leader: In love for our beloved church and in reverent memory
> of all those who by their services and sacrifices down through
> the years have bequeathed to us such a valuable church property;
> People: We burn this mortgage.
> Leader: In grateful appreciation of the generosity of the mem-
> bers and friends of this church the spirit of loyalty, unity and
> sacrifice manifested by the whole church in this achievement;
> People: We burn this mortgage.

PRAISE RESPONSE
> Holy, Holy, Holy, Lord God of Host
> Heaven and earth are full of Thee
> Heaven and earth are praising Thee
> O! Lord most high.

DEDICATION   (people seated and bowed)
> Leader: In determination that we shall enlarge our vision and
> that through its minister, its elders, its deacons and its other
> faithful leaders this church shall serve more effectively.
> People and Leader: We now dedicate ourselves, our services
> and our substance anew to the work of this our beloved church
> and to the extension of the kingdom of Jesus Christ throughout this
> community, this nation and the whole world that the will of God
> may be done on the earth as it is in heaven.

> (The treasurer of the Church will then burn the mortgage
> on a tray placed on the table near the pulpit)

> (It is wise to burn a substitute paper, rather than the actual
> mortgage itself, as a legal precaution. The underlying
> value is in the symbolic act, not the paper itself.)

DOXOLOGY

CLOSING PRAYER   (Chairman of the Building Committee)

A FAREWELL SERVICE OF AN OLD CHURCH BUILDING

> After conducting the morning service as usual, then follow with a farewell service in the old building.

THE MINISTER PRESIDING: This moment in the life of our congregation is mingled with thoughts of sadness and of joy. We regret to leave this old house of worship so sacred to our memories. At the same time we rejoice that larger and more suitable facilities are being provided that we may expand our service to others and provide for a growing family of church people. Let your hearts have right of way as we seek today in a fitting way to say good-bye to this building — this sanctuary.

THE CHAIRMAN OF THE CHURCH BOARD: This is a moment for which we have longed, yet as we come to the last good-bye our hearts burn within us. These four walls have housed our congregation for many years. Numbers of people have come and gone from this community, having found here their church home. We leave this property that we may meet the need for expansion and growth. In this we take courage and seek to follow the Master who leads on.

CHAIRMAN OF THE BUILDING COMMITTEE:
> (Note: This statement may refer to the new facilities, completed, or to temporary quarters in which the work of the church will be housed as the congregation awaits the dedication of a new building. Plans may be submitted in anticipation of dedication. An announcement of progress in fund raising may be included. Other items of an appropriate nature may be mentioned.)

A LITANY OF GRATITUDE AND JOYFUL ANTICIPATION

Minister: For the many years of service this church house has provided for this congregation, and for the hallowed associations we recall.

Congregation: We offer to Thee, our Father, a sincere word of gratitude.

Minister: For the children, youth and adults whose lives have been guided and enriched through the varied religious activities carried on in this church plant,

Congregation: We praise Thy name, O God, as we feel the Challenge of Christian growth.

Minister: For the devoted lives of ministers, musicians, Evangelists, elders, deacons, ministers of education, leaders among women, youth, children, men,

Congregation: We give Thee our word of deep gratitude.

Minister: For Christian liberality toward the erection of this building and for those who have in any way contributed toward the maintenance of this church home,

Congregation: We acknowledge with sincere gratitude.

Minister: For the new, enlarged and more suitable church home we are soon to enjoy, and, for everyone who has shared in this forward-looking enterprise, whether little or much,

Congregation: We would rejoice with hearts attune to songs of victory and achievement, and hope.

Minister: From hallowed memories of joy, of sorrow, of dedicated lives, the fellowship of kindred minds, shared in this old house which we "need no longer".

Congregation: We turn our hearts toward the hills of home in our new, beautiful, commodious, worshipful church home in which we today pledge to continue serving our Master with ever increasing faith, understanding and growth.

BENEDICTION: Jude 1:24, 25

— Adapted

PART III

DEDICATION OF THINGS

DEDICATION OF AN ORGAN

THE ORGAN PRELUDE

THE OPENING SENTENCE

THE INTROIT   (The Chancel Choir)

THE PROCESSIONAL HYMN: "O Come, All Ye Faithful"
(The congregation will be seated at the close of the hymn.)

THE INVOCATION AND THE LORD'S PRAYER

CHORAL RESPONSE

STATEMENT CONCERNING THE ORGAN   (Minister)

THE SERVICE OF DEDICATION

Minister: That the ministry of music in this Church may be to the glory of God, let us dedicate this organ.

People: To the glory of God, the Father Almighty, that we may more worthily worship Him, we dedicate this organ.

Minister: To the praise of Jesus Christ, the Savior of Mankind, at whose birth the angels sang, that our joy in Him may find more worthy expression, we dedicate this organ.

People: And to the Holy Spirit, in whose fellowship the discords of life are lost in the glorious harmony of God's love, we dedicate this organ.

Minister: That blessing and joy may come to all of the people — children, youth, adults — who have eagerly shared in the dream of this day, having gladly presented their gifts to make it a reality, we dedicate this organ.

People: That those who come to this House of Worship may be comforted in sorrow, strengthened in weakness and encouraged in despair, we dedicate this organ.

Minister: That all of the sacred rites of worship — the blessing of little children, the baptism of those who confess Christ as Lord, the celebration of marriage, the ordination of lives to Christian vocation, and the rites commemorating our beloved dead — may be solemnized in all the beauty of holiness, and that in every crisis God may be known to be a very present help in trouble, we dedicate this organ.

THE ANTHEM: "Psalm 150"

THE PRAYER OF DEDICATION   (The Minister)

THE CONGREGATIONAL HYMN: "Praise to the Lord, the Almighty"   (Standing, all stanzas)

THE ORGAN RECITAL   (The Organist)

THE RECESSIONAL HYMN: "Joy to the World!" (standing, all stanzas)

THE BENEDICTION (The Minister)

CHORAL RESPONSE

DEDICATION OF A SERVICE FLAG

PRESENTATION OF THE SERVICE PLAG (An Elder and Superintendent of the Church School)

Dear friends in Christ, we are about to dedicate this Service Flag in honor and remembrance of our relatives, friends, and fellow members who have answered the call of our country in her hour of emergency. We shall ever keep them in our hearts and remember them in our devotions. These are their names — (list names and read them).

DEDICATION VOWS

Minister: In order that we may not be unrighteous and forget the freedoms for which our fathers gave their lives —

People: We dedicate this service flag.

Minister: As a testimony to the fact that neither distance, nor death has dominion over our Christian fellowship —

People: We dedicate this service flag.

Minister: In recognition of the redeeming power of sacrifice and innocent suffering —

People: We dedicate this service flag.

Minister: As a pledge of lasting friendship, affection and gratitude to those of our own who have answered the call of our country —

People: We dedicate this service flag.

Minister: As a covenant that we, under God, shall do all that we can for the establishment of such peace and freedom and good-will throughout the earth that their service and sacrifice shall not be in vain —

People: We dedicate this service flag.

Minister: In the name of the Father, and the Son, and the Holy Spirit —

People: We dedicate this service flag and pray for that peace which passes all understanding.

DEDICATION PRAYER

— First Christian Church, Whitesboro, Texas

DEDICATION OF THE CROSS

(This ritual is designed to be used as a portion of a regular order of worship for Sunday morning.)

MINISTER: "God forbid that I should glory, save in the cross of our Lord Jesus Christ, by whom the world is crucified unto me, and I unto the world."

PEOPLE: That we also may likewise glory in the Cross of Christ and worship in the sight of it every Lord's Day, We dedicate this cross.

CHOIR AND CONGREGATION: "In the Cross of Christ I Glory"

MINISTER: "Then Jesus said unto his disciples, 'If any man will come after me, let him deny himself, and take up his cross and follow me.'"

PEOPLE: That we, beholding the cross may enter more truly into the mystery and power; We dedicate this cross.

CHOIR AND CONGREGATION: "When I Survey the Wondrous Cross" (first stanza)

MINISTER: "And Jesus said, 'The hour has come for the Son of Man to be glorified; and I, if I be lifted up from the earth, will draw all men unto me.'"

PEOPLE: That the cross may be lifted before our eyes, so that we, beholding it, may be changed from the satisfaction of self into the glory of self-sacrifice, we dedicate this cross.

CHOIR AND CONGREGATION: "Jesus, Keep Me Near the Cross" (first stanza and chorus)

Note: This dedication was used during a morning hour of worship by the Central Christian Church, San Antonio, Texas.

DEDICATION OF A PULPIT BIBLE

(For use preferably in a Sunday evening service)

ORGAN PRELUDE

INVOCATION

HYMN: "I Love Thy Kingdom, Lord"

SCRIPTURE READING: II Kings 22:8-17 (An Elder)

PRAYER

VOCAL SOLO: "Holy Bible, Book Divine"

WORDS OF PRESENTATION   (The Minister)

DEDICATION VOWS   (Led by a former Minister)

Minister: To the nurture of childhood, the evangelization of youth and those of mature years, and the encouragement of all who would serve the Lord,

People: We joyfully dedicate this Pulpit Bible.

Minister: To the spiritual enlightenment of all who worship with this congregation, and the complete spiritual furnishing of all who enter its fellowship,

People: We prayerfully dedicate this Pulpit Bible.

Minister: To the honored memory of men like Wycliffe, Tyndale, Coverdale, Luther and others who have sacrificed themselves to give us this "Word of Life" in our own tongue, and to the service of all those who use it in teaching and preaching the "Way of Life",

People: We humbly dedicate this Pulpit Bible.

Minister: To the glory of God, the Father; the exaltation of Jesus Christ our Lord and Savior; and to the indwelling of the Holy Spirit, through vigorous proclamation of his Kingdom among men,

People: We thoughtfully and hopefully dedicate this Pulpit Bible with a prayer on our lips and a song in our hearts. We rejoice now to renew our covenant toward right living day by day.

A MESSAGE FROM THE BOOK: Romans 12:1-21

PRAYER OF DEDICATION   (A guest Minister)

HYMN

OFFERTORY

PRAYER OF DEDICATION FOR THE OFFERING   (Chairman of the Church Board)

SPECIAL MUSIC

THE MESSAGE: "Holy Bible, Book Divine"   (Minister)

HYMN OF CONSECRATION: "Living for Jesus"

BENEDICTION   (Minister)

DEDICATION OF NEW COMMUNION WARE

INTRODUCTORY STATEMENT   (This may give name of donor, the occasion that prompted the gift, any other words of an appropriate nature.)

LITANY OF DEDICATION

Leader: In obedience to Him who said: "And when He had given thanks, He broke it and said: Take eat, this is my body which is broken for you; this do in remembrance of me."

People: We dedicate this Communion ware.

Leader: In remembrance of Him who said: "This is the New Testament in my blood; this do ye as oft as ye drink it, in remembrance of Me."

People: We dedicate this Communion ware.

Leader: As a living memorial to Him who said: "As often as ye eat this bread, and drink this cup, ye do show the Lord's death until he comes."

People: We dedicate this Communion ware.

Leader: As a testimony of the living Presence of Him who said: "I will not drink henceforth of this fruit of the vine, until the day when I drink it anew with you in My Father's Kingdom."

People: We dedicate this Communion ware.

Leader: As a means of Divine Grace, and as source of forgiveness and renewal of fellowship in Christ.

People: We dedicate this Communion ware.

Leader: In order that we may realize that we are a part of an unbroken Christian fellowship, and that we must dedicate ourselves anew to the work of His Church; so that our lives may be channels through which His Spirit may flow to others who may also share the salvation He brings.

People: We dedicate this Communion ware.

Used in the First Christian Church, Stanford, Illinois

DEDICATION OF AMERCAN AND CHRISTIAN FLAGS

PRELUDE: "America the Beautiful"

OPENING SENTENCE:

Blessed is the nation whose God is the Lord,
The people whom he has chosen as his heritage.
— Psalm 33:12

How precious is thy steadfast love O God!
The children of men take refuge in the shadow of thy wing.
— Psalm 36:7

HYMN: "My Country 'Tis of Thee"

PRESENTATION OF FLAGS (A statement by the donor, or someone representing this person)

ACCEPTANCE OF FLAGS (A timely word by some key person in the organization to which the flags are being presented)

STATEMENT ON THE SIGNIFICANCE OF THE AMERICAN
FLAG   (Leader)

HYMN: "The Star-Spangled Banner"   (Standing)

SALUTE TO THE AMERICAN FLAG   (Flag of the United
States)

> I pledge allegiance to the flag of
> the United States of America and to
> the Republic for which it stands,
> one nation under God, indivisable,
> with liberty and justice for all.

THE STORY OF THE CHRISTIAN FLAG:

All of us are interested in birthdays. We recall with interest
the story of the birthday of the flag of our nation. The birthday
of the Christian flag was September 26, 1897.

One Sunday, the Sunday school of the Brighton Chapel, Coney
Island, New York, was observing Rally Day. A special speaker
had agreed to come, but for some reason did not arrive. The
superintendent, Mr. Overton, made good use of the time by giving
an impromptu talk. The American flag had been draped over
the pulpit for the occasion, and the inspiration came to him that
the Sunday school and the church should have a special flag to
symbolize loyalty to God. In his talk he gave expression to this
thought.

The idea seemed worth following up, so Mr. Overton discussed
it with a well-known flag maker in the city. He made the first
Christian flag, which was used for the first time in the Brighton
Sunday school shortly afterward. Other Sunday school leaders
soon heard of it and were attracted by its beauty, simplicity, and
meaning. They began giving it publicity until now the Christian
flag is used around the world.

The field of pure white represents peace and purity. The field
of blue, the color of the unclouded sky, is a symbol of truth and
fidelity. The red cross signifies Christian service. The flag con-
tains no symbol of warfare. It is a symbol of no one race or nation
but includes all who bear the name Christian.

A national Flag is a symbol of a nation's ideals. The Christian
flag is the symbol of the Kingdom of God, from which these
ideals come.

— Adapted from *Worship and Hymns,* Bethany Press

HYMN: "Fling Out the Banner" — (One Stanza)   (All standing)

SALUTE TO THE CHRISTIAN FLAG:

> I pledge allegiance to the Christian

flag and to the Savior for whose
kingdom it stands, one Saviour crucified,
risen, and coming again with life and liberty
for all who believe.

CLOSING HYMN: "My Country, 'Tis of Thee" (Fourth stanza, to be sung thoughtfully as a prayer)

DEDICATION OF A BAPTISTRY

(This brief service is designed for use at the close of a regular morning or evening hour of worship in the sanctuary. The act of dedication is the actual use of the baptistry in administering the ordinance, to a group of candidates whose names should appear in the printed order of worship.)

HYMNS OF CONSECRATION AND COMMITMENT (All singing while the minister and candidates are preparing for the baptisms): "Take My Life and Let It Be"; "Where He Leads Me I Will Follow"; "O Jesus, I Have Promised"

MESSAGE: "The Meaning of Christian Baptism" (Minister)
(This brief message may be spoken by the minister from the baptistry, and, will include short quotations of Scripture such as Romans 6:4 and the story of the baptism of Jesus by John the Baptist.)

PRAYER:
Our heavenly Father, we have assembled here in the reverent quietness of this sanctuary to use for the first time our new baptistry. May this be a sacred moment to every one of us. We pray that through the subsequent history of this church this ordinance will be looked upon with awe and reverence. May the meaning of this symbolic act leave a lasting impression on the heart of these candidates and upon us all. As we in the administration of this sacred ordinance dedicate our baptistry, grant that our lives may be rededicated to serve the Master who said at his baptism, "to fulfill all righteousness." Keep us close to him, and forgive us when we falter. May thy guiding Spirit rest upon each of us in full measure. In his name. Amen.

BAPTISM OF CANDIDATES (List names here. Quiet music should be played as each candidate is baptized.)

CLOSING HYMN: "O For a Closer Walk With God"

Note: In churches where the mode is other than immersion a baptismal font may be dedicated.

DEDICATION OF A PIANO

(May be used in a small church. Will bear elaboration where desired.)

PRELUDE

PROCESSIONAL   (Congregation will stand as choir enters)

ASCRIPTIONS OF PRAISE

Minister:

Praise the Lord!
For it is good to sing praises to our God;
For he is gracious, and a song of praise is seemly.
— Psalm 147:1

People:

Sing aloud to God our strength;
shout for joy to the God of Jacob!
— Psalm 81:1

INVOCATION AND THE LORD'S PRAYER

CHORAL RESPONSE: "Threefold Amen" (Danish)

RESPONSIVE READING

Minister: Praise the Lord! Sing to the Lord a new song, his praise in the assembly of the faithful!

People: Let Israel be glad in his Maker, let the sons of Zion rejoice in their king!

Minister: Let them praise his name with dancing, making melody to him with timbrel and lyre!

People: For the Lord takes pleasure in his people; He adorns the humble with victory.

Minister: Let the faithful exult in glory; let them sing for joy on their couches.

People: Let the high praises of God be in their throats and two-edged swords in their hands . . . Praise the Lord!

HYMN

LITANY OF DEDICATION

Minister: Our Father, we rejoice today in the dedication of this instrument of music to the ministry of melody and harmony among all who assemble in this house of worship. May its tones declare the glory of God.

People: To thy glory and to the enrichment of the souls of men, we dedicate this instrument.

Minister: From the earliest periods of the world's history music has been a medium of worship. From the days of the crudest harps to our own time, the religious emotions of thy people have been stirred by the consonance of vibrating strings,

People: To Thee, O God, we dedicate this instrument as a medium of worship.

Minister: The souls of the master musicians have been poured out through the great hymns of the church, and the lives of men have been lifted with concord of sweet sound, and the ideals of institutions been sounded forth,

People: Therefore, O God, we dedicate this instrument to the appreciation of the highest and best in sacred music among thy people here.

PRAYER OF DEDICATION   (By a Musician)

PIANO SOLO: Variations of "Nearer My God to Thee" (Heads bowed in meditation)

MESSAGE: "We Worship"   (The Minister)

HYMN OF CONSECRATION: "O Jesus, I Have Promised"

CLOSING PRAYER   (unison)
> Let the words of my mouth
> and the meditation of my heart
> be acceptable in thy sight,
> O Lord, my rock and my redeemer. Amen.
>
> Psalm 19:14

DEDICATION OF A HYMNAL

PRELUDE: Medley of Great Hymns (preferably in same key)

RESPONSIVE CALL TO WORSHIP:

Leader:
> O sing to the Lord a new song;
> Sing to the Lord, all the earth!
> Sing to the Lord, bless his name!
> Tell of his salvation from day to day.
>
> Psalm 96:1, 2

Group:
> My heart is ready, O God,
> My heart is ready!
> I will sing, I will sing praises!
> Awake, my soul!
>
> — Psalm 108:1

Leader:
> Make a joyful noise unto the Lord,
> all the lands!
> Serve the Lord with gladness!
> > Come before his presence with singing!
> Know that the Lord is God!
> > It is he that made us, and we are his;
> We are his people and the sheep of
> > his pasture.
> Enter into his gates with thanksgiving,
> And his courts with praise!
> Give thanks to him, bless his name!
> > — Psalm 100:1-4

Group:
> For the Lord is Good,
> > his steadfast love endures forever,
> and his faithfulness to all generations.
> I will sing of loyalty and of justice;
> To Thee, O Lord, I will sing.
> > — Psalm 100:5; 101:1

HYMN: "O Worship the King"

INVOCATION (The Minister)

RESPONSE: (all remain standing while singing the refrain)
> Holy, Holy, Holy, Lord God of Hosts,
> Heaven and earth are full of Thee,
> Heaven and earth are praising Thee,
> O Lord, most High!

FESTIVAL OF SONG (Favorite and new hymns from the new hymnal)

OFFERING
  Sentence of Scripture
  Offering Received
  Doxology and Prayer of Dedication

STATEMENT ABOUT THE NEW HYMN BOOK (Choir Director)

LITANY OF DEDICATION
  Minister: To the services of our worship that they may be enriched by the singing of the hymns of the faith,
  People: We dedicate this hymnal.
  Minister: To the spirits of the sainted crusaders of the cross who found in the songs of heroic faith their challenge and their strength,

People: We dedicate this hymnal.

Minister: To the aging and the aged of our church whose thoughts of God and man have found expression in songs and hymns of faith,

People: We dedicate this hymnal.

Minister: To our Christian youth whose zeal and idealism may be rekindled and renewed by the challenge of the hymns of the church,

People: We dedicate this hymnal.

Minister: To the spirit of unity in the brotherhood of Christians, manifest in the universal singing of hymns,

People: We dedicate this hymnal.

Minister: To the end that our thoughts may be lifted upward in praise, thanksgiving, consecration, our wills be strengthened in active faith, and our lives be dedicated to the ongoing of the Kingdom of God around the earth,

People: We dedicate this hymnal and pray that we may forever sing the old, old, story of Jesus and his love with enthusiasm and understanding.

PRAYER OF DEDICATION   (All standing)

HYMNIC RESPONSE: (All voices)
   "Sing Them Over Again to Me"   (One stanza)

BENEDICTION: I Timothy 1:17   (Minister)

DEDICATION OF CHURCH PEWS

(Within a morning hour of worship)

OPENING MUSIC

CALL TO WORSHIP
   "Wouldst thou worship here today?
   Then softly step,
   And if from off thy feet thy shoes
   In reverence thou hast taken —
   To stand on holy ground
   And feel and know
   That God is near,
   That Christ awaits
   To help strong men to face the world;
   So — softly step,
   and bow thy head,

73

And come within to worship God.

— Selected

HYMN

OFFERING SERVICE
  Offertory Sentence
  Offertory
  Doxology
  Prayer of Dedication

COMMUNION SERVICE
  Hymn: "Be Silent, Be Silent"
  The Communion of the Lord's Supper
  Hymn: (Same as above)

RESPONSIVE READING: (Some appropriate selection from the hymnal, or a special selection printed in a folder prepared for the occasion)

THE MORNING PRAYER (Minister)

CHORAL RESPONSE

HYMN: "All the Way My Savior Leads Me"

LITANY OF DEDICATION
  Minister: To the worship of God the Father, the Author of our lives and the Moulder of our destinies,
  Congregation: We dedicate these pews.
  Minister: To the enrichment of life in this sanctuary where we so often meet,
  Congregation: We dedicate these pews.
  Minister: To the fine art of beauty, symmetry, comfort, and churchliness, in which we share the better things of life at God's hand,
  Congregation: We dedicate these pews.
  Minister: Toward the spirit of brotherhood, of Christian fellowship and goodwill in public assembly where members, friends and neighbors are gathered in worship,
  Congregation: We dedicate these pews.
  Minister: To the end that we may unitedly lift our voices in hymns of praise, in the reading of the Bible, in meditation during the sacraments, in prayers of thanksgiving, intercession and benediction,
  Congregation: We dedicate these pews, and on this joyful occasion rededicate ourselves toward an enlarged program of work, instruction, training, evangelism and stewardship within the life of this church in the outward flow of the Gospel of Christ.

PRAYER OF DEDICATION

RESPONSE: "Where He Leads Me I Will Follow" (refrain only, from memory)

BENEDICTION: II Timothy 4:22 (The Minister)

DEDICATION OF CHIMES

(This dedication may be conducted at the vesper hour, preceded by a concert of sacred music on the chimes, that the worshippers throughout the community may share the experience.)

HYMNS OF THE CHIMES (Sounding within and without the Church or Chapel, where possible)

ASCRIPTION OF PRAISE (in unison):
Praise the Lord!
Praise God in his sanctuary;
Praise him in his mighty firmament!
Praise him for his mighty deeds;
Praise him according to his exceeding greatness!
Praise him with trumpet sound;
Praise him with lute and harp!
Praise him with timbrel and dance;
Praise him with strings and pipe!
Praise him with sounding cymbals;
Praise him with loud clashing cymbals!

Let everything that breathes praise the Lord!
Praise the Lord!

— Psalm 150

HYMN

INVOCATION (The Minister)

CHIMES: "Finlandia" by Sibelius; or "Vesper Hymn" by Bortnainsky

RESPONSIVE READING OF SCRIPTURE
Minister: O give thanks to the Lord, for he is good,
People: For his steadfast love endures forever.
Minister: O give thanks to the God of gods,
People: For his steadfast love endures forever.
Minister: To him who alone does great wonders,
People: For his steadfast love endures forever.
Minister: O give thanks to the God of heaven,

People: For his steadfast love endures forever.
— Psalm 136:1-4, 26

GLORIA PATRI   (Standing)

THE STORY OF THE CHIMES   (Include name of donor, a description of this particular set of chimes, how they will serve this community)

LITANY OF DEDICATION

Minister: To the glory of God our Father, to Christ our Lord and Savior, to the Church wherein we share divine fellowship,

People: We dedicate these chimes.

Ministry: To the ministry of music for the souls of men, that they may feel the inspiration of melody, harmony and beauty,

People: We dedicate these chimes.

Minister: To the kindling of religious fervor through the thrill of rapturous sound as it carries the songs of the ages to the souls of men of today and tomorrow,

People: We dedicate these magnificent chimes, and humbly pray God's richest blessing on their use.

PRAYER OF DEDICATION   (Minister or Guest Minister)

RESPONSE: (Played on the chimes)   "Bow Down Thine Ear, O Lord"

   (The worshippers are requested to leave in silence at the close of the response. The chimes will continue to sound in a melody of familiar hymns and classical church music.)

DEDICATION OF A PULPIT

ORGAN PRELUDE: "Benedictus," — Max Reger

CHORAL INVOCATION: "The Lord Is in His Holy Temple"

CALL TO WORSHIP   (Minister)

RESPONSE BY CHOIR

PROCESSIONAL HYMN: "Holy, Holy, Holy"

INVOCATION AND THE LORD'S PRAYER

CHORAL RESPONSE: "Sweet Hour of Prayer"

ANTHEM: "Almighty God of Our Fathers"

WORSHIP IN TITHES AND OFFERINGS
    Offertory sentence
    Organ Offertory: "Come Restful Peace," Bach
    Doxology and Prayer of Dedication

76

RESPONSIVE SCRIPTURE READING

Minister: Jesus came into Galilee preaching the Gospel of the Kingdom of God, and saying, the time is fulfilled, and the Kingdom of God is at hand, repent ye and believe the Gospel.

The People: And Jesus went about Galilee, teaching in their synagogues and preaching the Gospel of the Kingdom.

Minister: And Jesus said unto his disciples, Go ye into all the world and preach the Gospel to every creature. He that believeth and is baptized shall be saved, but he that believeth not shall be damned.

The People: How then shall they call on Him in Whom they have not believed? And how shall they believe in Him of Whom they have not heard? And how shall they hear without a preacher?

Minister: For we preach not ourselves, but Christ Jesus the Lord; and ourselves your servant for Jesus sake.

The People: So shall my word that goeth forth out of my mouth; it shall not return unto me void, but it shall accomplish that which I please, and it shall prosper in the thing whereto I sent it.

LITANY OF DEDICATION

Minister: To the preaching of the Gospel of the grace of God, to the sounding forth of the word of the Lord, to the proclaiming of the will of God, speaking in the name of Christ to the people all the words of life,

The People: We dedicate this pulpit.

Minister: To the exaltation of Jesus Christ, the Son of God, the Way, the Truth and the Life; to the proclamation of His Lordship, to teach the observance of all things which he has commanded,

The People: We dedicate this pulpit.

Minister: To the memory of our beloved dead who gave their lives that we might enjoy liberty as children of God,

The People: We dedicate this pulpit.

Minister and People: We now, the people of this church and congregation, grateful for our heritage of truth, remembering the sacrifices of our fathers in the faith do dedicate this pulpit unto the proclamation of the pure word of God, that men may believe that Jesus is the Christ, the Son of the Living God, and that believing they may have life through His name.

HYMN: "How Firm a Foundation (One Stanza)

ANTHEM: "The Omnipresence," Franz Schubert

SERMON

INVITATION HYMN: "I Gave My Life for Thee"
COMMUNION SERVICE
  Hymn: "Lead Me to Calvary"
BENEDICTION   (The Minister)
CHORAL RESPONSE: "Peace"
ORGAN POSTLUDE
  Adapted from service used by the Central Christian Church,
  San Antonio, Texas.

DEDICATION OF AN ART GLASS WINDOW

PRELUDE: "Variation of Abide With Me", or " 'Tis Midnight in the Garden Now"
CALL TO WORSHIP   "The Lord is in his holy temple; let all the earth keep silence before him" (Hab. 2:20).
SILENT PRAYER   (The organ plays softly several prayer hymns)
PRAYER RESPONSE: "Threefold Amen"
SCRIPTURE READING: Matthew 26:30-46
DUET: "The Beautiful Garden of Prayer"
INTERPRETATION OF THE ART GLASS WINDOW
ACT OF DEDICATION
  Leader: To the development of a deeper sense of the devotional life,
  Congregation: We dedicate this window.
  Leader: To the memory of the Master who brought life to its fullest meaning as the expression of God's matchless love.
  Congregation: We dedicate this window.
  Leader: To the generous soul who made possible this wonder work of art, that all who worship here may drink in its silent message,
  Congregation: We dedicate this window.
  Leader: As the light of day reflects the perfected work of the master painter, the amazing skill of the artist who has brought this stirring message to us through his workmanship, may the Light of God's abounding love through Christ, forever challenge the sons of earth. In his name,
  Congregation: We dedicate this remarkable work of art with its silent message to the deepening of our prayer life.
PRAYER AND BENEDICTION

RESPONSE: "We Would See Jesus — for the Shadows Lengthen"
(One stanza by Choir)
POSTLUDE

DEDICATION OF CHURCH FUNDS
(Suggestion)

It is common practice in Protestant communions to receive the offering as an act of worship and to provide an orderly procedure for bringing the offering to the altar and dedicating it with a prayer. This is a vital part of the order of worship and is accompanied with a ritual in keeping with the practice of each communion, and local congregation.

A unique idea was inaugurated by Chaplain Charles M. Buck, while serving as minister of the Pecan Springs Christian Church, Austin, Texas. Working in cooperation with the stewardship and finance department of the church and convinced that giving may be an effective teaching experience he arranged for a dedication of the funds received for world outreach causes on the first Sunday of each month. The agencies and institutions of the brotherhood being supported by the church were listed for regular budget support on a weekly basis.

As the first Sunday of each quarter drew near, a letter and check were prepared for each of these agencies and institutions. These letters and checks were brought to the morning worship service. The minister, with the congregation reviewed each cause represented in the budget, the checks were placed in envelopes, and a prayer of dedication was offered.

In this way the congregation is continually aware of sharing in the World Task of the Church. (Each church using such a program would insert its own causes and amounts.)